CULTURE, CONSCIOUSNESS, AND BEYOND

An Introduction

Russell Crescimanno, Ph.D.
edmont Virginia Community College

VERSITY
SS OF
ERICA

LANHAM • NEW YORK • LONDON

Copyright ⓒ 1982 by

University Press of America,™ Inc.

**4720 Boston Way
Lanham, MD 20706**

**3 Henrietta Street
London WC2E 8LU England**

Library of Congress Cataloging in Publication Data

Crescimanno, Russell.
  Culture, consciousness, and beyond.

  Bibliography: p.
  1. Consciousness—Social aspects. 2. Left and right
(Psychology) 3. Self-fulfilling prophecy. 4. Educa-
tional psychology. I. Title.
BF311.C74 1982   303.3'2   82-17425
ISBN 0-8191-2811-2
ISBN 0-8191-2812-0 (pbk.)

Dedication

For Amy and Noah - that they may learn not to
confuse who they are with what they are labeled.

Acknowledgments

A theme developed throughout this work maintains that words are often less than satisfactory when it comes to expressing the essence of a human being or the "suchness" of life. This is especially the case as I attempt to thank all those whose help made possible the completion of this project. There are many, and I am grateful beyond words.

The following people were most immediately involved and to them, and the lessons that came through them, I extend my deepest thanks; Hal Burbach, Haqiqa Barricelli, Helen Clark, James Esposito, Peter Hackett, Virginia Jones, Phyllis Kleiber, Howard Kutchai, Mike McMahon, and Jennings Wagoner.

To my wife Lenette, for all the waiting and working, the growing and loving given throughout this "season" of our lives, and for typing and generally caring for the original manuscript from start to finish- I am, again, grateful beyond words.

TABLE OF CONTENTS

                                                  Page
PREFACE
    An Overview.   ix

INTRODUCTION.   xii

CHAPTER ONE
    Some Effects of the Academic Labeling
    Process.   1

CHAPTER TWO
    The Role of Language in the Social
    Construction of Reality.   15

        The Social Psychology of George
        Herbert Mead.   15

        Symbolic Interaction and the
        Labeling Perspective.   19

        The Sociology of Knowledge.   24

CHAPTER THREE
    Two Modes of Consciousness:
    The Split Brain in Man   29

        Left and Right Hemisphere Functions .   29

        Split Brain Research.   31

        The Active and Receptive Modes. . . .   34

        The Concept of Complementarity. . . .   37

        Two Realms of Consciousness:
        The "Ordinary" and "Non-Ordinary" . .   38

CHAPTER FOUR
    The Nature of "Ordinary" Consciousness . .   41

        A Recapitulation.   41

        Ordinary Consciousness as a
        "Stream" - of Words   42

        Ordinary Consciousness as
        Self-Consciousness.   43

Self-Consciousness and the Illusion
of Separation 45

Ordinary Consciousness:
In Need of a Change 50

CHAPTER FIVE
The Nature of Non-Ordinary Consciousness . 55

The Need for A New Image of Man . . . 55

The Complementary Nature of
the Two Perspectives. 57

The Automatization of Mind. 58

The Deautomatization of Mind. 59

Thought Watching: A Technique of
Deautomatization. 61

The "Field" of Consciousness:
An Organizing Principle 65

Common Characteristics of the
"Field" Experience. 68

The Transforming Nature of the
Field of Consciousness Experience . . 70

Conclusion. 72

BIBLIOGRAPHY. 77

AN OVERVIEW

Words as labels are the primary vehicle through which the human animal is introduced to the on-going world of meanings. This is a gradual process of becoming whereby human animality becomes civilized essentially by learning and internalizing the language structure of a society. In this way one's awareness is culturally conditioned, the house of one's consciousness is socially erected, but the scope and character of one's vision is necessarily focused and narrowed. Words introduce people to meaning, and to that end they are essential. Ultimately, however, they are the great delimiter of imagination and tend to keep people locked within the parameters of intellectual definition and description.

This inquiry is an effort to develop two major propositions. First, that the reality of everyday life is largely a social creation and the result of knowing the world through an intellectualized process of symbolic interaction. Knowing the world primarily through the intellect is largely a consequence of being immersed in a culture favoring a particular cognitive mode of adapting to the world which happens to be associated with the left cerebral hemisphere of the brain. It is through this hemisphere and this labeling, categorizing process that the flow of the world is segmented, broken up into bits and pieces, and thus understood. But in so doing, there is the tendency to lose sight (and feeling) of the fact that labels always refer to something beyond themselves and are merely convenient ways of pointing to reality and not that reality itself.

The second proposition suggests that this compartmentalized, intellectual perspective of reality is but one of two major modes of knowing the world available. The other, a more intuitive, holistic, culturally transcendent, and at times spiritual apprehension of the world and its events, now known to be associated with the activation of the right cerebral hemisphere, has largely been ignored and depreciated by socializing institutions generally--and educational institutions in particular.

In directing so much attention to the development of the intellect, schools have overlooked the intuitive dimension of human being and have thus addressed themselves to only one side of a living, multi-dimensional

self. In so doing, they tend to take the life out of
learning by confining it to the level of logic and
reason.

It is ever more apparent that to approach the
understanding of the world exclusively through the
intellect ignores the complexity and fine shadings
that constitute the "suchness" of life. The inadequacy
of this approach stems from its being incomplete and
thus inaccurate. In and of itself, the world is not
differentiated by hard and fast boundaries and in the
same sense people, in and of themselves, are not what
they have been labeled. There is simply more to it
all than that, more subtlety, more in the way of intricate integration, more complexity.

The structure of mind, it has been proposed here,
is bimodal in nature. There is the capacity to know
about the world through the intellect and the concepts
it generates which mediate the relationship between a
person and the objective world of events.

There is also the capacity to know the world
intuitively and directly, unencumbered by language and
thought. This involves an intimate communion with the
known that is deep and abiding and thus adds an essential quality or dimension of awareness to the epistemological process.

Rather than being at odds, these two modes of knowing actually imply and complement one another. To have
one without the other creates a state of deficiency and
imbalance that is dysfunctional and unnecessary since
mind is a holism that incorporates both. Clearly, it
is possible to have the best of both worlds where intuitive insight continually makes transparent the horizons created by the effort to describe and define the
human experience.

> Of all the hard facts of science,
> I know of none more solid and fund-
> amental than the fact that if you
> inhibit thought (and persevere)
> you come at length to a region of
> consciousness below or behind
> thought . . . and a realization of
> an altogether vaster self than
> that to which we are accustomed.
> And since the ordinary consciousness,
> with which we are concerned in ordin-

x

ary life, is before all things
founded on the little local self,
and is in fact self-consciousness
in the little, local sense, it
follows that to pass out of that
is to die to the ordinary self
and the ordinary world.

It is to die in the ordinary
sense, but in another sense, it
is to wake up and find that the
'I', one's real, most intimate self,
pervades the universe and all other
beings . . .

So great, so splendid is this
experience, that it may be said
that all minor questions and doubts
fall away in face of it; and certain
it is that in thousands and thousands
of cases the fact of its having come
even once to a man has completely
revolutionized his subsequent life
and outlook on the world.

(Edward Carpenter, 1844-1929, in
Ferguson, 1973)

INTRODUCTION

In the past ten years American educators have become increasingly aware that success and failure in school may have more to do with a phenomenon W. I. Thomas called the "self-fulfilling prophecy" (in Volkart, 1951) than with the assumed inherent ability of the student. Put simply, Thomas' dictum asserts that if people define situations as real, they tend to be real in their consequences.

In the context of the classroom, this suggests that the expectations and images which teachers and other school officials come to hold of a student are often the result of having defined and labeled the student's appearance, behavior, speech patterns, sex, race, social class, previous test scores and whatever additional "diagnostic data" are available. The concept of the self-fulfilling prophecy has drawn attention to the fact that these definitions and labels, conjured up and applied by the school and communicated to the student in one way or another, often function to create or perpetuate the very conditions they define.

In other words, it is becoming increasingly clear that something inherent in the very process of sorting out, labeling, and classifying students seems to simultaneously construct a network of "verbal rings" both around and within them. These metaphorical rings really represent the feedback acquired by the student in the process of negotiating his way through the school system and its expectations. One comes to learn about oneself in the context of the responses made by others. In this way, people accumulate information about themselves as learners, achievers, potential citizens, and even as humans with whatever measure of worth is doled out in the process.

If the feedback is basically positive and affirms the growth and growing potential of the person, if the verbal rings are polished golden, then they can and are used as toe holds or stepping stones to the proverbial better things in life. There is nothing magical about it. It is expressed in the form of self confidence, popularity, good grade reports, and a wide variety of abilities that largely spring from having been consistently defined and treated as one who is able.

When these same verbal rings are tarnished, whether through sheer neglect or through a thousand messages that all say one thing - "You're slow", "dull", "plain", or "average", the ultimate effect is to convince people that they are forever limited in this way and that their value and place in society is correspondingly limited. Consequently, it is becoming more and more apparent that by enclosing people in categories, both physical and mental, the stage is set for the actors involved to play-out the roles they have come to acquire.

Students, then, can come to be "typed" in much the same way that actors speak of being type-cast in a given role. Since this ultimately limits the scope and quality of their careers, forever being seen as a particular kind of character, many established performers go to great lengths to resist such typing - even if it means refusing to accept a part which they feel will only serve to cast them in the shadow of the type.

However, students (and perhaps aspiring young actors) do not enjoy the luxury of being able to refuse a role, at least not without suffering further complications arising from such resistance. Students generally do not have the power nor the insight that would allow them to intervene effectively in the process of academic stereotyping and say; "No, that's not me. That is a label or image you have created about me -- but that's not me." Consequently, the manner in which a person behaves and comes to feel about himself and his behavior depends to a great extent upon how it is others come to see and respond to him.

While educators are becoming increasingly aware of the self-fulfilling nature of the labeling process operating in the schools, there is little evidence that anyone knows what to do about it -- and for good reason. The process of labeling, and of people responding to what the labels imply, is something that goes on in every institutional nook and cranny of society. It is not something unique to school systems as such, but rather is an inherent aspect of all social systems. The way we come to know about the world we are born into is largely by learning the labels that have been assigned the various "things" in it, and the way these things are to be classified, compared, understood and used. The labeling process underway in the schools, then, is viewed here as a dramatic illustration of a much broader and more pervasive social process whereby people are taught to understand and know about the events of the world through a language and the meanings created by its words.

In focusing in on the labeling process as it occurs in the school system, one is afforded special insights into the delimiting effects that labeling has: both on children trying to make their way in the academic marketplace and, more generally, in desensitizing us to the realities of the world that exist apart from our definitions of it. A child who is labeled as "slow and troublesome" and consequently treated as a second-class citizen cannot be expected to value himself nor take stock in his own potential for growth. Yet who would deny that the reality of the child is missed entirely by these or any other labels? The essence of personhood lies beyond words and cannot be captured or contained by categories. Personhood contains limits as integral elements of the living organism; but labeling imposes limitations from without which are artificial and extraneous and stand in the way of self growth and discovery (Moustakas, 1977).

In spite of the growing awareness of the difficulties generated by this prophetic labeling process in the schools, two major problems remain unresolved and have stymied real insight and growth in the area. The first is that in the absence of a more expansive theoretical framework the notion of the self-fulfilling prophecy is relatively barren as an explanatory tool. In other words, it just does not take one very far in understanding our relationship with words as labels: why they are used as they typically are, the role they play in constructing impressions of the world, and what, if anything, can be done to alter this relationship. Ray C. Rist (1970) points this out succinctly in the following passage:

> The concept of the self-fulfilling prophecy has remained simply that -- a concept. The lack of a broader conceptual scheme has meant that research in this area has become theoretically stymied. Consequently, there has evolved instead a growing concern over the refinement of minute methodological nuances.

What is needed, then, is a theoretical framework with sufficient depth and breadth to give the bigger picture -- something that helps one to see how words as labels function in the general process of becoming socialized. Regardless of whether one is talking about people in educational institutions, mental institutions penal institutions or marital institutions, the results are seen to be the same. Because they define, labels also limit and these limitations tend to invite further labeling. Not until the role that language plays in the construction of both self and society is fully understood can educators begin seriously to consider intervening in any meaningful way in the dynamics of this process. The discussion here attempts to clarify this role.

The second problem is a natural outgrowth of the first. In short, people simply do not know how to (or even that they can) view others and their behavior free from the labels and categorical constraints they have learned to impose upon themselves so "naturally." Labeling is second nature to human beings. One is engaged in the process so much of the time that it is rarely realized that the world can be apprehended through some vehicle other than the words of a language.

This represents an effort to initiate solutions to these two problems; first, by offering a theoretical framework that explains academic stereotyping as simply one illustration of an absolutely pervasive social phenomenon which will simply be called "the labeling process" -- the dynamics of which constitute the very heartbeat of societal interaction. Secondly, by establishing both the theoretical and methodological groundwork that is necessary if people are also to begin to relate to one another at the level of being; which is to know each other holistically -- free from the confines of labels.

Essentially, then, this inquiry is an effort to develop two major propositions. First, the reality of everyday life is largely a social creation and the result of knowing the world through an intellectualized process of symbolic interaction. Knowing the world primarily through the intellect is largely a consequence of being immersed in a culture favoring a particular cognitive mode of adapting to the world which happens to be associated with the left cerebral hemisphere of the brain (Gazzaniga, 1967). It is through this hemisphere and this labeling, categorizing process that the flow of the world is segmented, broken up into bits and pieces, and thus understood. But, in so doing, there is the tendency to lose sight (and feeling) of the fact that labels always refer to something beyond themselves and are merely convenient ways of pointing to reality -- not that reality itself.

Leo Buscaglia (1972) recounted that while at Harvard Timothy Leary once remarked, "words are a freezing of reality." Echoing this sentiment Buscaglia suggested: "Everything that happens is filtered through this stuck, frozen system (of words), and that keeps us from growing. How many kids have not been educated just because someone pinned a label on them somewhere along the line?" It is precisely this process of creating and freezing realities with words that we are trying to explain and understand here.

The second proposition suggests that this compartmentalized, intellectual perspective of "reality" is but one of two major modes of knowing the world available. The other, a more intuitive, holistic, culturally transcendent, and at times spiritual apprehension of the world and its events, now known to be facilitated by activating the right cerebral hemisphere, has largely been ignored and depreciated by socializing institutions generally -- and educational institutions in particular (Bogen, 1969). However, by learning to uncover and examine the meaning-structures defining the "realities" of our lives with a dispassionate detachment, one can actually open the mind to new ways of perceiving and being in the world by experiencing a very different yet complementary dimension of consciousness. In this way, knowledge of our own complex selves and those with whom we are engaged is expanded immeasurably by broadening the base of awareness.

These two dimensions of consciousness, the intellectual - rational and the intuitive, have existed and been recognized since the dawning of mankind. Poets, philosophers, physicians, and metaphysicians have sung the praises of one or the other of these two perspectives for so long that one wonders if anything is to be gained by another voice joining the chorus. Traditionally, however, these two different modes of knowing have been set against one another in a variety of dichotomous battles. For example, the virtues of reason have been extolled above any involvement with the passions, or the way of science lauded over that taken by

religion. On the other hand, the spiritually inclined
have maintained that our attachments to the profane
world prevent us from seeing its illusory nature and
keep us from entering the realm of the sacred (Greeley,
1974).

That these two dimensions of consciousness have
historically been set apart and opposed to one another
actually reflects a cultural thought-pattern, a tendency to think in categorical terms of either/or rather
than any truth that these two ways of viewing the world
are mutually exclusive. As it is, people are generally
socialized into one, the intellectual-rational, and are
ultimately unable to see the world apart from the
labels and meanings their culture has created and imposed upon it.

The intent here is to introduce these two modes
of knowing as different yet complementary aspects of
a single field of consciousness. Both points of view
are necessary if one is to develop a complete picture
of reality since each reveals a measure of truth from
its own angle of vision. To look out upon the world
exclusively through one or the other frame of reference is to miss the other side of the coin completely,
something like insisting that the moon had but one
side because that is all one could see.

The human brain is clearly the most exquisite tool
available to mankind and yet so much of its known potential remains unexplored and untapped. The right
cerebral hemisphere has been identified as having the
capacity to facilitate a state of awareness wherein
one perceives and experiences a common ground of unity
and interdependence underlying the multiplicity of
forms and their differences otherwise noticed and
emphasized (Ornstein, 1972). In addition to celebrat-
ing individual achievement with its emphasis on the
respective worth of the resulting "winners and losers",
schools are in a position (indeed, some would say
have an obligation) to help students discover this
common ground of Being they share with their total
environment.

Our work here will be to see these two ways of
knowing, the intellectual and the intuitive, as capable of complementing one another, as going-with each
other and as being mutually available rather than
exclusive. Their respective development is considered
essential to the full self-actualization of an individ-

ual and something that schools can take the initiative
in both exploring and developing.

CHAPTER I

Some Effects of the Academic Labeling Process

When one examines a variety of literature related
to the concept of the self-fulfilling prophecy, it
becomes apparent that academic research has tended to
focus more on the effects of this process than on its
causes; effects which are the outgrowth of having
looked at people, but having seen only labels. This
literature combines to offer a testimony to the general
principle that socially created labels and expectations
distort perception so that it is never the person or
situation itself that one learns to encounter, but a
series of ideas and predispositions about them instead
(Rist, 1973).

The dynamics enlivening this principle in the
classroom are made all the more intense by the fact
that those with the labels and the formal authority to
apply them are a variety of very powerful adults.
Those on the receiving end are powerless by comparison
and, particularly in the elementary years, quite vul-
nerable to the labels being applied and inclined to
eventually internalize and become what they have been
labeled (Becker, 1963). The broader point here is a
social psychological truism. People generally become
who or what they are to themselves through a very
similar process of internalizing the information re-
ceived about themselves from others, particularly from
those whose opinions really matter. The boundaries
between self and others are more apparent than actual.
The senses help create the impression that people begin and end with their skin and that one is forever
separate and apart from another. But people are and
can be involved with one another's becoming to a much
greater extent than is typically recognized. The
common conception of man as an island unto himself is
a self-imposed limitation that the scientific community is increasingly coming to document (LeShan, 1974).

In this literature review the following themes
emerge: (1) that teachers and school officials make
judgments and hold expectations of students which are
influenced by a wide array of social characteristics
associated with the student; (2) that these judgments
and expectations can become self-fulfilling when transmitted, picked up, and reinforced by others in both the

1

school and other social systems; and (3) that this entire procedure is better understood when seen as one particular expression of a broader, ongoing process of societal labeling, the dynamics of which are culturally determined and condition, to a large extent, both how and what it is people come to know about their world and the events that make it up. It is this latter point that is the main concern of our discussion here.

In attempting to discover just what kinds of major social factors influenced teachers' evaluations of students, J. Johnson (1973) identified three: Students' prior performance; various social status characteristics; and current performance. Prior performance seems to include everything from past grades and test scores to notes exchanged by previous teachers and counselors. Social status judgments are the result of inferences made based on observations occurring in the context of the classroom as well as in communications with parents. A child's position on the socio-economic ladder is easily inferred from grooming habits style of dress, need for free lunches, and the information on enrollment cards. This is not to imply that teachers or school officials go out of their way to bias themselves. They are generally trying to "diagnose" or "place" their students and are not typically aware nor intend for such placement to be self-fulfilling and permanent. Often, however, it is.

The work of Rosenthal and Jacobson (1968) served to focus attention on what appears to be a strong relationship between the judgments and expectations a teacher has of a student, and the way they consequently come to relate to one another which tends to confirm those expectations. Their findings suggest that the positive expectations teachers developed about children presented to them as having been tested and identified as "intellectual bloomers" (when they were actually just randomly selected), clearly influenced the teachers to react differently (positively) toward them. The result was that, as a group, these children did perform better by the end of the year. Rosenthal and Jacobson make the following observation regarding the major theme of their work:

> Perhaps the most suitable summary of the hypothesis discussed in this paper has already been written. The writer is George

Bernard Shaw, the play is
"Pygmalion", and the speaker
is Eliza Doolittle:

'You see, really and
truly, . . . the difference
between a lady and a flower
girl is not how she behaves,
but how she's treated. I
shall always be a flower girl
to Professor Higgins, because
he treats me as a flower girl
. . . but I know I can be a
lady to you, because you
always treat me as a lady,
and always will." (in Rubin,
1974).

Following up on the work of Rosenthal and Jacobson, Brophy and Good (1970) attempted to examine the dynamics of the self-fulfilling prophecy in greater detail. Their research revealed that teachers demanded more from those students they had come to expect more of and were also inclined to reward these children with praise when they performed as expected. On the other hand, they appeared to accept the poorer performance from those students for whom they held low expectations and were less inclined to reward these children with praise when they did do well. In each case the quality of the relationship was altered by the expectations the teachers had come to associate with the two groups. Brophy and Good discovered that teachers allowed those students for whom they had high expectations more time to answer questions, praised them more often, and were generally less critical of them.

The effect of a teacher's expectations can spread out beyond the immediate teacher-student relationship and can shape the structure of classroom peer associations. Flanders and Havumaki (1960) demonstrated that when teachers praised some (randomly selected) students and ignored others, this had a dramatic influence on the nature of peer relationships that emerged in the classroom. Those students who were looked upon favorably by the teacher were also more popular with their classmates. Those who had been relatively ignored were treated similarly by their classmates.

3

The ideas people have in their heads about other people (even if they are initially incorrect) shape the way they behave toward them which in turn sets the tone and direction of how it is the other will respond in return. If one is generally caring and supportive and sends out messages that are encouraging, people typically respond to the challenge and live up to the expectations (expecially children). This is why it is so essential that teachers be aware of both the source and the specific content of the expectations they hold of particular students or groups of students.

This is not as easy to accomplish as it may sound. Teachers' expectations are structured by a whole host of influences from standardized test scores (Goaldman, 1971), to the physical attractiveness of the students themselves.

Clifford and Walster (1973) hypothesized that a student's attractiveness strongly influenced a teacher's judgments of the child's intellectual and social behavior. In essence, the more attractive the student, the more inclined in his favor the teacher was expected to be. They concluded that:

> There is little question but
> that the physical appearance
> of a student affected the
> expectations of the teachers
> we studied. Regardless of
> whether the pupil is a boy
> or girl, the child's physical
> attractiveness has an equally
> strong association with his
> teacher's reactions to him.

Closely related to this theme has been the work of Brown (1968), Davidson and Lang (1960), Rubovitz and Maehr (1973), Rist (1970), Stein (1971), and a number of others who have examined the influence of race and ethnicity as powerful factors that shape the expectations teachers hold of students. Teachers tend to expect less of lower-class children than they do of those from middle class and consequently come to anticipate less in the way of achievement from the minority group members over-represented there.

The point here is that on the basis of these judgments students are labeled and classified into particular groups or tracks and are generally related to on

he basis of the "type" of person or student they have
een prejudged to be. This is the essence of stereo-
yping and the reason it is such a superficial and ul-
imately damaging mode of relating. The expectations
hat create the typification are transferred to the
ther, gradually internalized, and thus have the power
o be self-fulfilling.

Charles Silberman (1970) brings the crunching im-
act of this process to light as it comes to bear on
he schoolchild. In the following anecdote from Crisis
n the Classroom the dynamics of the self-fulfilling
rocess are made painfully clear.

> Three children are in a special
> class -- children with perceptual
> problems. The teacher insists on
> talking with the visitor about
> the children in their presence,
> as though congenital deafness
> were part of their difficulty.
> 'Now, watch, I'm giving them
> papers to see if they can spot
> the ovals, but you'll see that
> this one' - he nods in the di-
> rection of a little boy - 'isn't
> going to be able to do it.' A
> few seconds later, he says
> triumphantly, 'See, I told you
> he couldn't. He never gets
> that one right. Now I'll put
> something on the overhead pro-
> jector, and this one' - this time
> a nod toward a little girl - won't
> stay with it for more than a line.'
> Five seconds later, with evident
> disappointment: 'Well, that's the
> first time she ever did that. But
> keep watching. By the next line,
> she'll have flubbed it. The child
> gets the next one right, too, and
> the teacher's disappointment mounts.
> 'This is unusual, but just stick
> around . . .' Sure enough the child
> goofs at line five. 'See, I told
> you so."

Expectations thus provide the basis for classify-
ng and categorizing people while the category-as-label
ventually comes to establish one's expectations. In

other words, there is a cyclical movement to the entire
process which can be seen as having both negative and
positive poles. While it is true that most people
experience a combination of both, there is a tendency
for each individual to accumulate a preponderance of
experiences at one or the other end of the continuum.

Schmuck and Schmuck (1974) comment on the effects
of having more negative experiences.

> The student who more often
> experiences the negative cycle
> feels under stress and is
> anxious about his adequacy.
> He frequently distorts and mis-
> perceives others' reactions,
> tending to distrust or to dis-
> believe favorable feedback.
> Such destructive misperceptions
> keep the student from breaking
> out of the negative cycle. As
> years go by and such experiences
> pile up, it becomes more dif-
> ficult to make alterations in
> very negative self concepts.

In 1969 Makler examined a variety of schools in
Harlem and discovered that children had a tendency to
remain in the track in which they were originally
placed. It is becoming clearer, however, that such
placement is influenced by a variety of social factors
which have little to do with the actual ability of
students. Labels produce a "freezing" of reality!

The work of Rist (1970, 1972, 1973) is particularly effective in outlining the cumulative effects of
the self-fulfilling prophecy generated by the taken-
for-granted application of school labels. In a long-
itudinal study of a segregated elementary school in
the black community of St. Lous, he discovered that
after only eight days of kindergarten, the teacher
assigned permanent seats to students based on assumed
variations of academic ability. However, no formal
evaluation of the children had occurred! Assignments
to one of three tables were made on the basis of socio-
economic criteria so that the stratification of the
classroom came to reflect the stratification patterns
of the "street." The poorer children from welfare
families all sat at one table while working class and

middle class children sat at the other two. Rist show-
ed how the various expectations the teacher had of
these groups were manifested in terms of teaching time
devoted to each, the use of praise and control, and
the extent of autonomy within the classroom. He reports that:

> By following the same children
> through the first and second
> grade as well, I was able to
> show that the initial patterns
> established by the kindergarten
> teacher came to be perpetuated
> year after year. By second
> grade, labels given by another
> teacher clearly reflected the
> reality each of the three groups
> experienced in the schools. The
> top group was called the 'Tigers',
> the middle group the 'Cardinals',
> and the lowest group, the 'Clowns.'

Thus, the evaluations and expectations teachers
come to hold of students are made on the basis of much
more than mere ability. What happens to the growth
potential of a student, for example, when he is known
basically in the context of the label "slow learner"
or "clown?" One finds that the light of truth regarding his personhood is obscured by the shadow which
the label has cast. In this mind-set teachers tend not
to deal with the person as potential, as unique being
in the process of becoming, but are encouraged instead
to treat students as classified objects and to mistake
the meaning of a label for the essence of a person.

It is apparent that expectations and judgments are
the social "stuff" out of which labels are made. They
both reflect and create the underlying value structures
which provide the basis for the processes of judging
and evaluating. Indeed, people's views of the world
are clearly value-laden and nowhere is it necessary to
be more cognizant of this than in institutions of teaching and learning. The consequences of remaining insen-
sitive to the effects of school valuing and labeling
are monumental. In the next several pages the observations of a number of social researchers and theorists
create a perspective of the broader effects that are
generated by this process. They spread out from the
school and eventually function to maintain existing
patterns of social stratification. Labels are indeed

7

a freezing of reality.

Cicourel and Kitsuse (in Sieber and Wilder, 1973) maintain that the classification of students, for example, as college-qualified or non-college-qualified, is "a consequence of the administrative organization and decisions of personnel in the high school." In this way, the school occupies a strategic labeling position in the social system and can thus critically affect the life-chances of those it processes.

Cave and Chesler (1974) suggest that when we examine the relationship between the American school and social systems, we observe that the school re-inforces the norms and values of economically advantaged societal groups. They maintain that "operating as a primary preparation system for the socio-economic system, the school is largely responsible for perpetu-ating the myths associated with education, income, and social role and the resultant social class and status division."

For instance, a major socio-cultural value in American society is couched in the ideology of capital-ism with its resultant stress on maximal profit and achievement motivations. It is safe to say that through the medium of competitive achievement, meaning and pur-pose are derived for much of the population, to say nothing of material comfort and success. Cave and Chesler conclude that a focus on achievement inevitably promotes systems of inequality. These values are re-flected in our schools in the emphasis placed upon academic achievement and performance. Those who, for whatever reasons, do not manifest these values are typically labeled and seen as "deviants" to be watched, or as "casualties" to be passed along, rechanneled, or ejected from the system. This creates a large resi-due of marginal and alienated youth who have been de-nied an early and critical badge of success in the system. And it is the system, of course, which must ultimately absorb the disenchantment and dismay that comes from the perception that one's life-chances have been frozen.

Jules Henry (1963) makes a number of powerful ob-servations in his examination of the destructive con-sequences emanating from the competitive, achievement-oriented stance so overwhelmingly taken by the schools. Henry describes an incident that occurred during a fifth grade math session. Boris is at the blackboard

8

aving difficulty reducing a fraction to its lowest
erms. The teacher indicates that he should "think."
he classroom is transformed into a sea of waving
ands as other children strain to be first to demon-
trate that they know what Boris obviously does not.
iving up on Boris, the teacher acknowledges Peggy
ho is able to solve the problem. Henry comments:

> Thus Boris' failure has made
> it possible for Peggy to succeed;
> his depression is the price of
> her exhilaration, his misery
> the occasion for her rejoicing.
> This is the standard condition
> of the American elementary
> school . . . Somebody's success
> has been bought at the cost of
> our failure. To a Zuni, Hopi,
> or Dakota Indian, Peggy's per-
> formance would seem cruel beyond
> belief, for competition, the
> wringing of success from some-
> body's failure, is a form of
> torture . . . Yet Peggy's action
> seems natural to us; and so it
> is. How else would you run our
> world? And since all but the
> brightest children have the con-
> stant experience that others suc-
> ceed at their expense, they can-
> not develop an inherent tendency
> to hate - to hate the success of
> others, to hate others who are
> successful, and to be determined
> to prevent it. Along with this,
> naturally, goes the hope that
> others will fail.

Perhaps the most devastating consequences of the
lucational labeling process, then is that particular
eople and groups of people come to know in advance
hat academic rewards and success are not to be real-
stically expected. In the face of this, what be-
omes unrealistic is the expectation that high levels
f educational achievement can be generated and sus-
ained within such groups. This entire situation is
ompounded for lower class youth by the fact that
lternative opportunity structures are often as re-
tricted as the various educational avenues.

9

Commenting on this, Cloward (in Cave and Chesler, 1974) makes the following observation:

> Thus they experience desperation
> born of the perception that their
> position in the economic structure
> is relatively fixed and immutable -
> desperation made all the more poig-
> nant by their exposure to a cultural
> ideology in which failure to orient
> oneself upward is regarded as a
> moral defect and failure to become
> mobile as proof of it.

All that is being recounted here can be seen as an outgrowth of a labeling process that is certainly not confined to the classroom. For the fact is that people indeed look out at the world through a glass darkly. And this darkness is a result of the indiscriminate use of a process of labeling which stands, as it were, between the observer and whatever is being observed. Labels are the vehicles through which people learn to categorize and typify their experience and thus come to know the meaning of events in their lives. But in imbuing labels with meaning, one comes to freeze reality; forcing that which is alive and changing to be treated as inanimate and rigid, and forever.

Thomas Scheff (1975) discusses the ramifications of labeling both in the context of societally induced madness, and as a more ubiquitous social phenomenon.

> The attitude of labeling is to
> reduce the complex individual
> with many attributes and an
> eventful biography to a single
> descriptive trait. A person is
> defined exclusively by some single
> aspect of his character of behavior.

> The process of labeling may
> be seen as giving rise to a master
> status that excludes all other
> statuses from consideration . . .
> Categorization of persons is a
> pervasive, indeed ubiquitous
> process in modern society.

This is the way, then, that most people come to know most of what they know. We inherit a language

10

name is to know." The labels people acquire and apply both structure and infuse meaning into their lives so that one comes to apprehend the world from this or that particular point of view. However, this view is often obscured by the very labels used to see and understand what it is that is going on in the world. Assigning a number of students to a group labeled "the clowns" may serve some administrative end in the classroom, but any benefit is negated immediately if that label prevents anyone from taking those people's needs and interests seriously.

Clark E. Moustakas (1977) has commented in depth on the power of the labeling process to encourage a stifling conformity and a fear of the unknown. The individual is coerced into living his life in terms of the "shoulds" and "oughts" handed down by significant others and increasingly comes to loose touch with himself. Movement, in this case, is in the direction of self-alienation.

> In labeling, the individual is
> fixed so that reality is not
> experienced or known. Often
> the person loses touch with who
> he or she is and becomes the label.
> When we call others dumb or stupid
> or lazy, we are stamping them with
> that characteristic just as directly as if we were clubbing and severly
> injuring them. Labels are missiles
> that undermine and restrict or
> pressure a person to stray toward
> conforming to others' definitions
> and standards. (Moustakas, 1977).

To fully understand (let along change) the dynamics of labeling operating in the schools, a theoretical framework must first be developed which is capable of accounting for the entire range of societal labeling that occurs. An explanatory framework is needed that explains language and its labels, generally, as the vehicle through which realities are socially constructed - both in and out of the school setting.

The chapter that follows is an effort to shed more theoretical light on the problem of labeling than can be generated by an isolated concept like the self-fulfilling prophecy. Major theoretical tenets

11

and its labels and the associated meanings that others have assigned to the events of the world and, over time, come to take these entirely for granted. The consequences of being socialized into the reality of everyday life in this way are dramatic indeed. For the deleterious effects of the labeling process do not spring from the mere act of labeling or categorizing itself. In fact, classifying is an essential element in the process of abstract, conceptual thought. The harm done by the labeling process is a consequence of the tendency to forget that the label or category is actually <u>an abstraction people have created</u>; and the related inclination to behave as though the label, and that which has been labeled, are one and the same. Caught up in the dynamic, one comes periolously close to mistaking the menu for the meal!

Walter Lippman's discussion of the pictures in our minds which distort perception of reality is especially germane to the theme being developed here.

> (We do not first see, then
> define, we define first and
> then see . . . We are told
> about the world before we
> see it. We imagine most things
> before we experience them. And
> those preconceptions, unless edu-
> cation has made us acutely aware,
> govern deeply the whole process
> of perception. They mark out
> certain objects as familiar or
> strange, emphasizing the differ-
> ence, so that the slightly
> familiar is seen as very familiar,
> and the somewhat strange as sharply
> alien (Lippman, in Schur, 1971, p.40)

The point being developed here is that labeling in the schools, and all that goes with this, can be bet-ter understood when seen as a particular expression of a much more pervasive social process of labeling-through-language, a process through which all the events of the world are defined and categorized before they can hold any meaning for people.

In other words, the labeling that goes on in schools can be seen as a specific illustration of a more pervasive epistemological process wherein individ-uals are each taught that, directly or indirectly, "to

12

will be drawn from the social psychology of George
Herbert Mean (1934), the symbolic interactionist and
labeling perspectives which evolved from Meadian
thought (Manis and Meltzer, 1972), and the sociology of
knowledge, a persepective that arose from the phenomeno-
logists Husserl (1931, 1965), and Schutz (1962), and
was later developed sociologically by Manheim (1936),
and then Berger and Luckman (1967). This theoretical
blend makes a significant contribution toward the
development of an integrative explanatory model, a
perspective which offers a clear understanding of the
social dynamics involved in both the origin and maintenance of the labeling process. From this theoretical
vantage point it is possible to assess what needs to
be done to disentangle ourselves from the webs that we
tend to weave with words. One can learn to use the
mind to go beyond the mind, to see beyond the limitations that the labels impose. But first, it is essential that one acquire the thorough understanding of
just how it is that language itself manages to structure so much of our thinking and very being in the
world.

CHAPTER II

The Role of Language
In The Social Construction of Reality:

Three Theoretical Perspectives

To understand the phenomenon of labeling in the schools, or anywhere else for that matter, it is necessary to develop a thorough understanding of the function of language in the general process of knowing. It is important to realize the extent to which people rely on language to negotiate their way through the world and its relationships. People come to know and understand their worlds largely in terms of the names and associated meanings that events are assumed to "have." The three theoretical perspectives taken up in this chapter develop this theme and leave little doubt as to the impact of language on the mental and social worlds of any human being.

The Social Psychology of George Herbert Mead

From the social psychology of George Herbert Mead (1934) one can clearly see the extent to which words are the wings of meaning. Without them, how would people express what they know? How would they know what to express? Indeed, how would people know that they are people? Mead makes it abundantly clear that the labeling process is an essential component in even the most rudimentary development of the mind and self of any individual. Language-labels are inextricably involved in one's very sense of being from birth until death. Labeling that goes on in the schools, then, represents only a particular phase of a person's exposure and involvement with a process which continues throughout the life-cycle.

In Mead's social psychology, human behavior is not static nor fixed but rather a dynamic affair which is constantly in flux and always in the process of becoming. In opposition to the behaviorists of his day, Mead maintained that behavior is not released from humans as a result of "colliding" with environmental stimuli. Rather, the human organism is continually adjusting, creating, and recreating the various lines of action comprising any given social act. He does this as a result of taking his world into account

15

through the interpretive vehicle of a language system (Mead, 1934; and Strauss, 1956).

From the field of developmental psychology we are given to understand that the newborn infant's conception of itself is loose and without firm definition. Consciousness in the newborn appears to be undifferentiated to the point of precluding any developed distinction between self and mother; between the infant suckling, for example, and the mother from whom he draws sustenance (Greeley, 1974). In the beginning, then, one can assume that consciousness is essentially non-discriminating and the world and its "parts" are, for the infant, of a single whole.

But the function of society is to immediately begin to impress upon the newborn the multitude of labels and their meanings which people have created in an effort to compartmentalize, and thus make sense of, the otherwise continuous flow and flux of the world (Berger, 1967). The process of creating the discriminating mind is formally inaugurated by labeling (naming) the infant. In this way the first great dichotomization of the world is initiated and beckons the embryonic emergence of the self. Forever after there is always "me", and that which is "not me."

The emergence of a sense of self in the individual is the result of an interplay between the biological and social dimensions of the human organism (specifically, the development of the neo-cortex in the brain which allows for the reflexive activity so essential to thought - Mead, 1934) and one's involvement with others in a social context. Moreover, an individual is in constant interaction with himself in the course of interacting with others. Mead maintained that the behavior an individual displays in a given situation is typically the consequence of an ongoing dialogue between the individual as a subject ⊷ reflecting back on himself as an object. For an individual ". . . enters his own experience as a self or individual, not directly or immediately, not by becoming a subject to himself, but only insofar as he first becomes an object to himself just as other individuals are objects to him in his experience. . ." (Mead, 1934). What is more, Mead argued, the fullest development of the reflexive sense of self only occurs in the presence of language and meaning. Specifically, it is the verbal gesture or spoken word that enables us to objectify thoughts and feelings and to respond to ourselves as objects in our own experience.

> Reason cannot become impersonal
> unless it takes an objective, non-
> affective attitude toward itself;
> otherwise we just have conscious-
> ness, not self-consciousness, and
> it is necessary to rational conduct
> that the individual . . . should
> become an object to himself. For
> the individual organism is obviously
> an essential and important fact or
> constituent element of the empirical
> situation in which it acts; and with-
> out taking objective account of it-
> self as such, it cannot act intelli-
> gently or rationally. The importance
> of what we term 'communication' lies
> in the fact that it provides a form
> of behavior in which the organism or
> the individual may become an object
> to himself (Mead, 1934).

Mead developed the concept of role taking in an effort to clarify the developmental dynamics associated with the emergence and maintenance of a conception of self. Role taking involves a mental process wherein the individual anticipates and rehearses a variety of potential reactions his behavior may elicit from others and adjusts or continues his action on the basis of these predicted responses. In other words, the individual responds to himself as he expects others will. In this way he is able to construct his behavior so as to respond to, if not meet, the expected (or unexpected) demands of a situation.

> Language is the significant vocal
> gesture which tends to arouse in the
> individual the attitude which it
> arouses in others; and it is this
> perfecting of the self by the gesture
> which mediates the social activities,
> that gives rise to the process of
> taking the role of the other . . .
> (Mead, 1934).

In this manner people come to look upon themselves with some degree of objectivity and are thereby afford-ed a unique and essential control over their behavior.

17

This, as Mead points out, clearly underlies the dramatic distinction between consciousness and self-consciousness, a distinction that is rooted in the capacity to create and apply labels or language. Mead emphasizes that the emergence of a fully reflexive self is vitally dependent upon language as the vehicle that ultimately allows the individual to engage himself as an object,

This perspective makes it clear that people become aware of themselves as social objects through a constant communication process which involves making meaningful indications to one's self and others. Language-labels are, on the one hand, indispensable to the process of becoming a fully socialized and functioning societal adult. On the other hand, it is apparent that the indiscriminate application of labels can have a dramatic stultifying effect on the potential for human being. Once again, one is reminded of the need for a theoretical framework capable of accounting for both the positive and negative effects of the labeling process; something that helps one understand why labeling so often occurs societally as a "necessary evil."

The thrust of Mead's writing was to articulate a social theory of mind and self, to establish both their origin and development within the context of society. He maintained that the social significance of human behavior evolves from the fact that we do not simply respond or react to the actions of others. Rather, our actions are typically based upon the intentions and implications (the meanings) which we _infer_ from the behavior of others.

For example, if at some point in a heated discussion, one person closes his fist and draws back his arm, the other's reaction, whether it is to fight or take flight, is not a response elicited by the original act as such. Instead, it is a response to what the act implies, that is, that one is about to be struck. From the Meadian point of view, the meaning of any stimulus (gesture, sign, symbol or object) arises with the response to that stimulus and as such establishes a relationship that is mind. The essence of mind, then, is meaning while the essence of meaning arises out of language and relationship - out of the social field of interaction wherein it is constituted.

People are dependent on language for their most fundamental sense of self because it is language that

18

gives birth to meaning. Regardless if one is referring to what it means to add two and two and get four, or the meaning of the question "Who am I?", words as labels are generally the carriers of meaning which is why people are so dependent upon them in relating to and knowing about the world.

It bears repeating that the thrust of Mead's writing was to develop a social theory of mind and self, to establish both their origin and development within the context of language and society. It is within the interactions making up what Mead calls the field of mind that the meaning structure of a society is created, maintained, and ultimately transformed. For Mead and the symbolic interactionists who followed him, it is language or labels that give expression to thought-systems which, in turn create our realities.

From the first sensation of self, to the fullest understanding of society, language provides the building blocks out of which the house of one's consciousness is erected. This is why the labeling that is done, whether inside or outside of the schools, is done so matter-of-factly and typically taken for granted.

Symbolic Interaction and the Labeling Perspective.

Following the position developed by Mead, humans are seen as reflective, interactive beings who develop selves as a result of possessing the necessary physiological equipment (e.g., brain structures), and then being immersed in the organized company of others - society. From the interactionist point of view, the study of human behavior begins with the observation that human association is absolutely necessary for full human growth and development. For out of association emerges language and from language there arise shared meanings which create, in turn, the fundamental ground of societal being (Strauss, 1964). It is the articulation of this inextricable interdependency between self and others, between personality and social structure mediated by language, that identifies symbolic interaction as a distinctive school of thought. From this perspective, individuals cannot be fully understood apart from the social setting or situation wherein their action is considered meaningful.

W. I. Thomas (1931) considered the capacity to make decisions from within rather than having them

19

imposed from without to have been one of the most important powers acquired during the evolution of animal life. He stressed the significance of definitions of situations in the process of creating the self.

> Preliminary to any self-determined act of behavior there is always a stage of examination and deliberation which we may call the definition of the siutation. And actually not only concrete acts are dependent on the definition of the situation, but gradually a whole life-policy and the personality of the individual himself follow from a series of such definitions (Thomas, 1931).

Traditionally, the gap between the individual and society is seen as being bridged by the various processes of socialization. This is the manner in which man in society comes to manifest society in man (Berger, 1967). To identify the process of socialization as the link between individuals and larger social arrangments is to identify the procedure whereby meanings are constructed, maintained, and transformed through symbolic interaction.

From the symbolic interactionist perspective, the process of becoming socialized in society is largely a process of learning the names associated with various societal "games" (i.e., interlocking role performances) and thus coming to be "in the know." More broadly, people rely on definitions of situations to locate themselves meaningfully and negotiate their way through the reality of their everyday lives.

> Humans live in a world of objects that is not merely given in nature, but in whose construction they participate, via their symbols, and which is, at least in principle, a malleable world, rather than a fixed one. This is so chiefly because objects do not have meanings that are either intrinsic to them or merely learned and reflexively applied as people act toward them. Instead, the meanings of objects and thus our actions toward them,

20

are largely determined in the
course of our interaction with
others (Hewitt, 1976).

It is noteworthy that Hewitt qualifies his state-
ment regarding the malleability of the symbolic world
of man by indicating that this is so at least in
principle. In practice, however, people seem to fre-
quently suffer from a perceptual rigormortis that comes
with the mindless, taken-for-granted application of
old labels to new people and situations.

Symbolic interaction does not occur in a social
void but within the context of concrete, recognizable,
and labeled social surroundings. Human interaction is
always situated and can be seen as occurring within
"circumstantial containers" which have generally been
defined in advance of any given individual's involvement in the situation. The point to be underscored
here, and the essence of what has come to be called
the labeling perspective, is that the direction and
quality of any ongoing interaction is dramatically
affected by the definitions of the situation being
employed by the people involved.

The labeling perspective first took identifiable
form in the area of deviant behavior (Becker, 1963).
However, its major tenets really represent the back-
bone of social psychology and can be simply stated as
follows: How a person feels about himself and what he
does, depends to a large extent upon the kind of responses others made to both him and his behavior. Deviance, then, is not simply the result of discrete and
absolute acts of wrongdoing. More than anything else,
perhaps, it reflects the expression of very powerful
patterns and processes of social definition and stig-
matization.

Howard Becker (1963), is generally credited with
initiating the development of the labeling point of
view. He maintains that:

> The central fact of deviance is
> that it is created by society.
> I do not mean this in the way it
> is ordinarily understood, in which
> the causes of deviance are located
> in the social situation of the
> deviant, or the social factors,

21

which preempted his action. I
mean, rather, that social groups
create deviants by making the
rules whose infraction constitute
deviance, and by applying those
rules to particular people and
labeling them as outsiders. From
this point of view, deviance is
not a quality of the act the person commits, but rather a consequence of the application by others
of rules and sanctions to an
"offender." The deviant is one to
whom the label has been successfully
applied. Deviant behavior is behavior that people so label.

The thrust of this approach, then, is to develop
an understanding of deviance not as a static entity
emanating from some "bad apple," but as a continuously
constructed and reconstructed outgrowth of overt and
covert processes of social-symbolic interaction.

The labeling process is especially systematized
and institutionalized in school systems. The observation that schools are largely middle class institutions
staffed by middle class personnel espousing middle class
values and norms is relatively commonplace. That, as a
result of this, the stage is set for thousands upon
thousands of young people to be officially defined and
labeled as "failures", "rejects", "neer-do-wells", or
what have you is not as commonly realized. Perhaps
the most debilitating, self-defeating effect of the
labeling process is the illusion of fixity and perman-
ence this creates in a world clearly characterized by
temporality and change. In labeling the world there is
also the tendency to define it once and for all.

Much of the importance of the
definition of the situation in
human affairs arises from the
configurational element involved
in the process. When a situation
has once been seen in a particular
configuration, it tends to be seen
in the confinguration ever after,
and it is very difficult to see it
in any other. The configuration first
established may be said to inhibit

22

the formation of other configura-
tions (Waller, in Stone and
Farberman, 1970).

A primary function of the label-as-category, then
is to convert actions that occur in time, into ever-
lasting qualities of the being of the one who is categorized. Thus, because on this, that, and the other
occasion Johnny talks back to his teachers the conclusion may be drawn that Johnny is a "troublemaker."
However, the general implication is that he always will
be as well.

In his treatment of "labeling madness", Thomas
Scheff (1975) maintains that the process of labeling
generally gives rise to a master status that tends
to exclude all other statuses from consideration. It
is this exclusion of the possibility of change, inherent in the act of labeling, that makes the process so
deadening.

> The key to the labeling-denial
> continuum, it seems to me, is the
> process of defining a person as
> essentially and only a deviant.
> Compare the attitude of denial
> contained in the description,
> 'George drinks like a fish, but
> he is a talented, compassionate,
> and accomplished man,' with the
> attitude of labeling expressed
> in the statement, 'George is
> nothing but a drunk.' The attitude
> of labeling is to reduce a complex
> individual with many attributes and
> an eventful biography to a single
> description trait. A person is
> defined exclusively by some single
> aspect of his character of behavior
> (Scheff, 1975).

The process of knowing through labeling is something people are engaged in nearly all of the time. In
fact for many, the notion of knowing the world in some
way other than through labels is so foreign as to sound
absurd - so convinced are people that to name is to
know. However, it is increasingly coming to be acknow-
edged that the labeling process may be as problematic
in society as it is convenient. Many are realizing

that when substantial numbers of people feel that they are at a dead end, that they have been dismissed as "losers" and see no realistic way out of the circumstances making up their lives, that they are in but not of the society going on around them, - then they tend toward alienation, anomy, and the disenchanted fragmentation of the social order.

The theoretical perspective known as the sociology of knowledge has made major contributions to our understanding of the social dynamics through which labeling as-stereotyping structures people's interactions. While it helps one to see the omnipresent constraints imposed by socio-cultural systems, it also serves as a reminder that what man has created can also be changed.

The Sociology of Knowledge.

If the significance of Mead's work lies in the notion that mind and self are social products that emerge through the vehicle of language, and the importance of symbolic interaction has been to establish the mediating role that language plays as it "filters" our perceptions, then the major contribution of the sociology of knowledge lies in its assertion that, consequently, the reality of everyday life is a socially constructed affair.

Following Berger and Luckman (1967), the sociology of knowledge has as its primary concern an analysis of the processes whereby "reality" is socially created. It begins with the observation that the temporal, organizational relationship between the individual and society is such that prior to any particular individual's existence there is, already ongoing, an established social system. This is to say, one encountered a socially organized world that has been defined and interpreted prior to and independent of the individual's entrance on the social scene. The social essence or cement of collective life, then, lies in the definitions of situations, (the meaning structure of a society), which contribute so profoundly to the construction of what is called "the reality of everyday life."

It follows that great care is required in any statements one makes about the 'logic' of institutions. The logic does not reside in the institutions and their external

24

functionalities, but in the
way these are treated in reflec-
tion about them. Put differently,
reflective consciousness super-
imposes the quality of logic on
the institutional order.

Language provides the fundamental superimposition of logic on
the objectivated social world. The
edifice of legitimations is built
upon language and uses language as
its principal instrumentality
(Berger and Luckman, 1967).

In other words, one does not really stand a chance
in the dyadic interchange between individual and society.
There is simply no way for people to escape the crushing
impact of the social order, especially as it is impress-
ed upon them through the early formative and developmental years. People are shaped and molded by this pre-
established order whether they are aware of it or not.
The only freedom in the matter(a theme developed in the
following chapter) comes as a result of first realizing
the extent to which the mind has been conditioned, and
then learning to employ a neglected side of the brain
to initiate a state of consciousness that transcends
the limitations imposed by language and culture. Otherwise, we are forever society's children destined to act
out the constructed realities of our lives.

This reality of everyday life is perceived as both
orderly (i.e., prearranged in anticipated patterns), and
objectified (i.e.,as being out there or external) and
as such has tremendous influence over the individual.
The vehicle through which meanings are predominantly
transmitted to societal newcomers is language. Thus,
learning the language of one's socio-cultural system
implies learning the meaning structures which have come
to be associated with it. Learning the one implies
learning the other - they arise mutually. Language is
thus a social fact and enjoys the same experiential
status as physical facts. That is, one encounters it
as external and constraining or coercive in its effects.
It has incredible power. It has the power of convention
to force thinking, behavior, and experience into pre-
established patterns.

This social construction of the reality of every-

25

day life proceeds on the basis of two related principles with vast implications for the understanding of labeling as a specialized form of knowing.

The first is that social life is a dynamic affair springing from the flexible give and take of ongoing, fact-to-face interactions. This dynamism, however, is simultaneously circumscribed by the interpretive meaning structures, known as <u>typification schemes</u>, (Berger and Luckman, 1967), which condition the manner in which people apprehend that which presents itself to them in the world. In other words, people appear to one another and understand each other in terms of "types." Language, then, functions to typify experience and in large measure people negotiate with each other and the world through these various typifications. Thus, for example, the other appears to me as "a student", "an inarticulate student", and so - "a lousy student." These typification schemes are, of course, reciprocal and the other apprehends me as "a teacher", "a disapproving teacher", and thus "a lousy, prejudiced teacher." In a manner of speaking, then, these schemes, these ideas of the mind, enter into negotiations with one another. Berger maintains that they occur in the context of broader <u>situational typifications</u> which define particular actions, thoughts, and feelings as either appropriate or inappropriate for a given situation.

The second related principle involved here maintains that the consequence of these typification patterns is to <u>routinize</u> our interactions so that much of the reality of everyday life becomes <u>taken-for-granted</u> and unquestioned once cast in the rigid mold of the type*(Schutz, 1967).

It is in this way that the labeling process tends to become a self-fulfilling prophecy. Labeling can be taken for granted to the extent that one is not inclined to question the validity, appropriateness, or even the need for applying this process to a given situation. Instead, there is the generalized assumption that "to name is to know" and this assumption is drilled into us from the day we are born.

*The sum total of these typifications in all their manifest variability, and the recurrent patterns of interaction established by means of them, becomes the social structure of a group and a profound social fact of its organized existence.

26

These meaning structures are transmitted to the societal newcomer through the socialization process and are, by and large, internalized. This process of socializing the young is initially enacted by significant others, typically parents, with whom children are highly emotionally identified. The significance of this emotional bond is especially apparent when one recalls the extent to which children are open and receptive to the definitions of situations offered by their parents. Significant others thus mediate or "filter" the social world on the basis of the particular interpretive or definitive point of view they have acquired as a result of going through the same process.

Knowing the world through these various labeling categories provides us with a relative, conditioned view of events, rather than a knowledge of the nature of things in and of themselves. In other words, it is rarely the reality of people or things exactly as they are that one sees and knows, but only these realities as conditioned by various modes of seeing and understanding.

> Symbols, then, are stimuli
> with learned meanings. They are
> the foundation not only of every-
> day social life, but of human
> civilization. They derive from
> specific social contexts in the
> course of interaction. As this
> suggests, symbols form the basis
> for our cognitive processes generally
> and for our overt behavior . . . .
> We can only understand the world
> in terms of the symbols that are
> available to us or in terms of
> symbols which we create to explain
> the world. The latter is rare, how-
> ever. For the most part, people
> accept the world in terms of the
> language they learn (Lauer and Handel,
> 1977).

What people learn from and about, then, are a series of judgments made about a network of appearances, not about the people or things that appear. It is like being at a play and becoming so taken by the set, lighting, costumes, and lines being spoken that one forgets the entire drama has been staged to create the appearance of reality. Similarly, the world appears to us dressed in the various costumes that labels provide. We say, for example, that "a snowflake has a pattern" - or - "it is raining" and in so doing come to accept unthinkingly that there are two distinct "things" existing in each case. In this way the structure of language and its associated meanings (created realities) prevent us from realizing that the snowflake is the pattern and that without any "it" as the cause, there is simply rain.

Language thus makes the world appear as it does in this or that linguistic guise. It organizes the world by dividing it, and then defining and categorizing the things it has created within it. The sociology of knowledge concludes that knowledge is relative, both in terms of its dependence upon categorization, and the fact that any given set of categories only manifests or arises against a particular cultural overlay or back-drop. Each person, then, lives out his life largely within the constructed realities imposed through societal consensus and decree. But this is not an immutable condition that mankind must simply learn to live with.

Knowledge through labeling is merely one way of knowing the world! And perhaps its most potent con-sequence, the perpetuation of the social stratification system, can be seen as the inevitable result of a state of mind that knows no other way of knowing; a condition of mind that is ignorant, for example, of a more expansive perspective which makes apparent the inherent synthesis of parts with the whole. From this perspective the world is experienced as an integrated whole, free from the artificial distinctions created by culture.

The capacity for this kind of holistic knowing is inherent in the human organism as organism and resides, more specifically, in the intricacies of the right cerebral hemisphere. The following chapter explores two major modes of knowing which are associated with the left and right hemispheres of the brain. Intellectual knowledge, identified with the left hemisphere, is the kind of knowledge described in this chapter: it is lingual and linear and culturally limited in terms of the information it provides. Intuitive knowledge, on the other hand, is holistic and culturally transcendent and the right hemisphere from which it springs may well represent the one key capable of unlocking the doors of our perception.

CHAPTER III

Two Modes of Consciousness:

The Split Brain In Man

Growing up in society really means largely having the contents of one's consciousness both created and arranged. It has been argued thus far that this content is basically made up of language - words, labels, categories, definitions and meanings. Most people live their lives in verbal realities that have been socially constructed and never come to realize that there is another world, another realm of consciousness that has nothing to do with words and labels. As research in the psychology and physiology of human consciousness sheds increasing light on the mysterious structure and function of the brain, some researchers are beginning to realize the extent to which people have neglected a side of themselves with literally awesome capabilities for awareness that transcend the limitations of language and meaning imposed by culture. There are two distinct modes of consciousness that exist and are available. Knowing the world and its people through labels is only one of them.

Left and Right Hemisphere Functions

Although the notion that two distinct modes of consciousness exist is centuries old, it is a relatively recent discovery that this bi-modality is grounded in the physiology of the human organism. Through the work of Ornstein, 1973; Gazzaniga, 1967; Diekman, 1971; and Bogen, 1969; in the area of neuropsychiatry, it has been discovered that there are two epistemological sides to the human organism which are related to the left and right hemispheres of the brain. The labeling, categorizing mode of knowing which was taken up in the second chapter, is identified with the intellectualizing, active left side of the brain and represents the manner in which people organize most of the data they encounter into information to assist them in negotiating their everyday lives.

Especially in adults, the left cerebral hemisphere is characterized by linear-rational processes. It tends to filter sensory input and to limit, select, and discriminate amongst all the available data and to isolate that which it considers important.

29

In other words, it tries to be
logical. It works like a digital
computer and strings relevance into linear, logical messages. It
is fed by the skills of reading,
writing and arithmetic because
they are linear forms of communication (Samples, in Allman and
Jaffe, 1976).

This method of knowing is used almost exclusively
in educational (and all other) institutions; to the near
total exclusion of the intuitive, non-linear, right
hemisphere of the brain through which one can acquire
a more intuitive, tacit knowledge.

The left hemisphere, then, appears to be specailiz-
ed for analysis while the right seems to excell in holistic mentation. In this state of mind one focuses not
on the parts of anything as parts, but on their inex-
tricability instead — on the ineffable composure of the
whole. The language ability of the right hemisphere is
quite limited, which accounts for the difficulty typically experienced when trying to find "the right words"
for an intuitive feeling-state. This is also why particular experiences associated with right hemispheric
activity, hallucinogenic or mystical-religious experiences, for example, are so often defined as ineffable -
as being beyond words.

The right hemisphere is largely responsible for
one's spatial orientation and is also called into expression in creative work associated with arts and
crafts. The nature of its involvement in the coordina-
tion of behavior seems to demand of it the ability to
integrate a variety of input from the environment at
once. It operates simultaneously or holistically rather
than sequentially, as the left hemisphere does. It has
the ability to formulate patterns and to create gestalts
which provide the basis for its potential and the unique
contribution it offers to consciousness (Samples, in
Allman and Jaffee, 1976).

It is increasingly coming to be realized that both
modes of knowing are available to people because they
are directly associated with the biological "baggage"
that we inherit. However, our culture is primarily
verbally or intellectually oriented and thus has tended
to neglect the tacit, intuitive dimension of knowing

30

argely because it has labeled that knowledge as being
oo sujbective, imprecise, unscientific and unreliable.
n addition to a genetic factor involved in the deter-
ination of cerebral dominance, Roger Sperry (in Annual
ditions, 1978) makes clear the role that the culture
lays in the process.

> . . . our educational system and
> modern society generally (with
> the very heavy emphasis on com-
> munication and on early training
> in the three Rs) discriminates
> against one whole half of the
> brain. I refer, of course, to
> the non-verbal, non-mechanical,
> and spatial mode of apprehension
> and reasoning. In our present
> school system, the attention
> given to the minor hemisphere of
> the brain is minimal compared
> with the training lavished on the
> left, or major, hemisphere.

n the other hand, there is a growing agreement among
ubstantial segments of the scientific and lay commun-
ties that the tacit dimension, far from being insignif-
cant and inferior, "is an essential component of man's
ighest capabilities" (Ornstein, 1973).

lit Brain Research

The brain is essentially a double organ consisting
f two hemispheres joined by a bundle of interconnected
erve tissues called the corpus callosum. Some twenty-
ive years ago, researchers at the University of Chicago
iscovered that when the corpus callosum (of a cat) was
evered, each hemisphere performed independently as
hough it were a whole brain (Sperry, et al. 1969).
rom this rather startling discovery there emerged sev-
ral new and heuristically profound questions for those
nvolved in brain function research. Was the corpus
allosum responsible for integrating the operations of
he two hemispheres? Or, conversely, would cutting the
orpus callosum in humans result in a dissociation, of
orts, of the two sides of the brain? To what extent
ould they actually function independently when separ-
ted? If there is the possibility of there being "two
inds" available, are they each capable of registering
eparate thoughts and emotions?

31

Roger Sperry and his co-workers (1969) at the California Institute of Technology have been involved in some remarkable research which begins to address these questions directly. As a result of their work with experimental animals indicating that severing the corpus callosum did not seriously damage mental capabilities, surgeons were encouraged to perform similar operations on patients afflicted with severe epilepsy. They were trying to restrict the seizure to one hemisphere. The surgery proved to be so successful that Sperry and his associates suspected the intact callosum of actually facilitating seizures in these patients.

Michael S. Gazzaniga and his associates (in Ornstein, 1973) have conducted a number of experiments with some of these patients. They noted that while the day-to-day affairs of these "split-brain" people suffered little if any impairment as a result of the surgery, subtle tests they devised clearly revealed that they had succeeded in separating or holding apart the specialized functions of the two cerebral hemispheres. Their research has made immense contributions to the understanding of human consciousness.

The tests they devised to determine the extent to which separation of the hemispheres had affected the mental capacities of the brain were ingenious. One was visual, the other tactile. In the visual experiment a picture of some written notation was presented for a fraction of a second to either the left of the right cerebral hemisphere. In the tactile experiments a variety of objects, kept from the subjects' view, were placed in either the right or left hand. This again insured that the information was being presented to just one hemisphere at a time. It is important to keep in mind that the left and right hemispheres of the brain control the right and left sides of the body respectively.

Gazzaniga commented on the results of the tests:

> When the information
> (visual or tacitile) was presented
> to the dominant left hemisphere,
> the patients were able to deal
> with and describe it quite nor-
> mally, both orally and in writing.
> For example, when a picture of a
> spoon was shown in the right visual
> field or a spoon was placed in the

32

right hand, all the patients
readily identified and described
it. They were able to read out
written messages and to perform
problems in calculation that
were presented to the left hemisphere. In contrast, when the
same information was presented
to the right hemisphere, it
failed to elicit such spoken
or written responses. A picture
transmitted to the right hemisphere evoked either a haphazard
guess or no verbal response at
all. Similarly, a pencil placed
in the left hand (behind a screen
that cut off vision) might be
called a can opener or a cigarette
lighter, or the patient might not
even attempt to describe it. The
verbal guesses presumably come not
from the right hemisphere but from
the left, which had no perception
of the object but might attempt to
identify it from indirect clues
(Gazzaniga, in Ornstein, 1973).

Gazzangia is quick to point out that this impotence
of the right hemisphere does not mean that the surgery
had reduced its mental abilities to a moronic level.
Rather, when the researchers asked for nonverbal answers
to the visual and tactile tasks presented in their tests,
the right hemisphere in a number of their patients dis-
played a significant ability to perform accurately.

For example, when a picture of a spoon was shown to
the right hemisphere, the patients would feel around
with the left hand, sorting through a variety of objects
kept from their sight, and identify a spoon as a match
for the picture. The researchers continued to find
evidence of the ability of the right hemisphere to function on a par with the left, expecially when it was free
to operate outside of the world of words. It is becoming increasingly apparent that the designations "major"
and "minor", so often used to label the left and right
hemispheres respectively, are misnomers born of ignorance - the result of having misunderstood and ignored
the non-verbal contributions of our other half.

Gazzaniga and his associates discovered, for example, that the right hemisphere was also capable of generating _emotional_ responses.

In one particularly fascinating experiment a variety of ordinary objects was passed before the visual field of the subjects. Suddenly, a picture of a nude woman was flashed. It made no difference which of the two hemispheres saw the picture - the subject was amused in either case. The only difference was in the ability to say what one had seen. When flashed to the left hemisphere the person would laugh and verbally identify the picture as that of a nude. When flashed to the right, and asked what they had seen, they would say that they had seen nothing! But almost immediately a sly smile or some related expression would spread across their faces and they would begin to laugh. When asked what they were laughing at they would say things like "I don't know, nothing . . . oh - that funny machine." Even though the right hemisphere could not verbally express what it had just seen, it did elicit an emotional response to the nude like the one the left hemisphere had given. (Gazzaniga, 1967).

This split-brain research has generated one major and very powerful conclusion: that separation of the two hemispheres results in the emergence of two independent spheres of consciousness within one organism. Sperry maintains that the data coming from the research in this area leads to the conclusion that splitting the hemispheres splits both the brain _and_ its psychic properties. He writes that "Everything we have seen so far indicates that the surgery has left each of these people with two separate minds, that is, with two separate spheres of consciousness" (quoted by Bogen in Ornstein, 1973).

Gazzaniga goes so far as to assert that "It is entirely possible that if a human brain were divided in a very young person, both hemispheres could as a result separately and independently develop mental functions of a high order at the level attained only in the left hemisphere of normal individuals" (1967).

The Active and Receptive Modes: A Complementary Relationship

It is known that there are two distinct modes of consciousness available and that they are directly related to the functional properties of the left and right hemispheres of the brain. Moreover, it appears that humans have the ability to alternate from one mode to the other depending upon the nature of the activity required in a particular situation. Perhaps the most significant outcome of current research, however, has been the realization that these two modes of knowing complement and, in so doing, complete one another.

Arthur Deikman (1971) has advanced our understanding of the complementary nature of these two modes considerably. He identifies left hemispheric activity with what he calls an action mode, while the activity of the right hemisphere reflects a receptive mode. Both, however, are required for the full functioning of the human organism.

The action mode of the left hemisphere is an orientation designed to help one manipulate the environment. Accordingly, then, the main psychological expression of this state reflects focal or narrowed attention, sensitivity to boundary perception, and a preference for shapes and meanings rather than colors and textures. In general, this mode of perception seems to notice the trees rather than the forest. Deikman comments:

> The action mode is a state of
> striving, oriented toward
> achieving personal goals that
> range from nutrition to de-
> fense to obtaining social
> rewards . . . Sharp perceptual
> boundaries are matched by sharp
> conceptual boundaries, for suc-
> cess in acting on the world re-
> quires a clear sense of self-
> object difference. Thus, a
> variety of physiological and
> psychological processes develop
> together to form an organismic
> mode, a multidimensional unity
> adapted to the requirements of
> manipulating the environment
> (Deikman, 1971).

Language, Deikman asserts, "is the very essence of the action mode." As was noted throughout chapter two, language is the vehicle through which the world is compartmentalized; that is, broken up into bits and pieces which can then be grasped, both physically and psychologically, and ultimately acted upon. In the course of

35

human growth and evolution the action mode takes prece-
dence for assuring biological survival. This is not to
imply that the receptive mode does not also develop, but
rather that it develops in the space or interval between
what are increasingly longer periods of action-mode
functioning. It is not surprising, then, that people
develop a cultural preference for the action mode and
consider it to be especially appropriate for adult life.
Unfortunately, this occurs at the expense of receptive
states which are often dismissed as irrelevant, or depreciated as pathological and regressive. Current research in the psychology of human consciousness, however, has been instrumental in helping to correct this
jaundiced view.

Rather than manipulation of the environment, the
receptive mode of the right hemisphere is an orientation
centered around its intake. Diffuse rather than focused
attention characterizes this state along with a "melting"
and harmonizing of sharp boundary distinctions. This
entire mode appears to be designed for absorption of the
environment - for a profound integration of the self
with its environmental field. As a result, this hemisphere of the brain is capable of initiating experiences
that reveal an underlying unity as the fundamental ground
of being from which everything else arises. As in Martin
Buber's I - Thou relationship, one is picked up and
immersed in the "currents of universal reciprocity"
(Buber, 1970). The receptive mode allows a person to
engage the world in its own context, as an end in and of
itself. Rather than intervening, one is interwoven; and
instead of encountering, one is engaged.

> Characteristically, the relation-
> ship to the environment in the
> receptive mode is what Buber (1958)
> describes as the "I - Thou," in
> contrast to the 'I - It' of the
> active mode . . . . The receptive
> mode is not a 'regressive' ignoring
> of the world or a retreat from it
> - although it can be employed for
> that putpose - but is a different
> strategy for engaging the world,
> in pursuit of a different goal
> (Deikman, 1971),

It is important not to think of these two modes of
knowing as "active" and "passive" in nature and therefore opposed to one another, Both represent different

36

forms of activity sutied to different goals and purposes:
In some situations people are required to act on their
environment, while in others they are asked to take it
in. In Deikman's works, "'Letting it' is an activity,
but a different activity than 'making it'."

In our society people are virtually obsessed with
making it and seem to have little sense or appreciation
of the underlying harmonies that integrate them with
their physical and social environments. One tends to
be saturated with the psychology of becoming and consequently sees nearly everything as a means to some
future end. Just being, at one with what is, is an
experience too often depreciated as unproductive, or
scheduled for vacations and retirement.

The experience facilitated by the right hemisphere,
experiences of being rather than becoming, are the natural complement of those associated with the left. However, people are not accustomed to the concept, let
alone the experience, of complementarity and so tend to
find it initially contradictory if not confusing. But
it may well be that man's continued survival as a species will depend upon the extent to which the peoples
of the world are able to cultivate a genuine appreciation of the dynamics of integration and cooperation inherent in the principle of complementarity.

The Concept of Complementarity

Our culture tends to associate passivity with meek-
ness and inferiority and something, therefore, which
should be combatted, something against which one sets
himself. This is why it would be mistaken to conceptu-
alize this bimodal movement of mind as an active-passive
dichotomy at odds with itself. Instead, the principle
in operation here is Niels Bohr's concept of complementarity (1958), where polar opposites function not to op-
pose one another, but to integrate and **complete** each
other.

The concept arose in physics when light was observed to behave in what appeared to be a conflicting manner
when viewed under different conditions. On some occa-
sions it assumed the characteristics one associates with
particles; while on others, it behaved more like a series
of waves. The principle of complementarity allows for
the integration of these apparently divergent views by
incorporating them both in a description of the reality

37

of light.

> After complementarity in physics
> had been accepted, it was realized
> that observations which give con-
> flicting (complementary) views of
> phenomena cannot, when taken by
> themselves, be accepted as complete
> nor, therefore, as totally correct
> descriptions of nature. . . . .
> Only the complementary description
> is completely and, to the best of
> our knowledge, correct (Blackburn,
> in Ornstein, 1973).

This is how one is encouraged to understand the
relationship between the two hemispheres of the brain,
the modes of consciousness associated with them, and
the different views of reality that each yields. They
are complements - not combatants. In other words, it
is not an either/or situation, but one in which each
completes the other. People are in the position to ex-
pand immeasurably the horizons of their world view simply by acknowledging and developing both of the cerebral
gateways that open onto it. Because they complement one
another, their fullest integration and development often
takes the form of extraordinary achievement and creative
expression.

Two Realms of Consciousness: The "Ordinary" and the
Non-Ordinary"

The intuitions capable of being initiated by the
right hemisphere lead one to a sphere of consciousness
which Rollo May (1953) calls creative consciousness of
self. While this is something that will be treated
more fully in the last chapter, for now it is enough to
indicate that this is a non-ordinary state of mind characterized by sudden insight, the "dawning of ideas", and
the experience typically thought of as inspirational.
"As all students of creative activity make clear", he
says, "this level of consciousness is present in all
creative work."

The problem, of course, is that most people experience this quality of mind only rarely - if at all. So
engrossed are human beings in the realities created with
words that one literally learns to discount the possibility of seeing things in any other way. For most people,
unfortunately, the creative consciousness of self repre-

sents a potential rather than actual experience, since one is taught to approach and understand the world largely through the activities associated with ordinary left hemisphereic functioning. A person's apprehension of the world-about-him is overwhelmingly a process of learning the language-labels that have been applied to the people, places, and events which comprise the reality of one's everyday life. A rather startling consequence of this one-sided view of the world is that people are always (at least) one step removed from reality. The world comes to us second hand, as it were, because what is "out there" is first filtered through a language-meaning system which has been so thoroughly internalized in the process of socialization that one simply cannot conceive of any other way of knowing.

This self-imposed limitation is all the more unfortunate in view of the vast unfolding potential available in the development of what amounts to a complementary mode of consciousness. As it is, however, the nearly exclusive reliance on labels to bridge the gap between one's self and the world has, at the same time, cultivated a sense of separation and apartness from that very world. It is as though in trying to describe the world, people tend to distance themselves and somehow miss it!

The following chapter takes a closer look at this experience of separateness and identifies it as the predominant characteristic of ordinary, everyday consciousness. The consequences associated with approaching and experiencing the world exclusively from this frame of reference are profound. People are affected at every level of organized being, biological, psychological, and sociological.

Summarizing, then, we can say the following. The human organism is blessed with a cerebral capacity far beyond that which is typically utilized. More than suggesting a deficiency in the quantity of what is known, failure to develop the intuitive potential of the right hemisphere represents a loss in the depth or quality of knowledge developed and transmitted by a culture. The holistic mentation available through right hemispheric perception introduces another dimension to thought and experience that both complements and completes the epistemological process. Michael Polanyi (1967) has called this the "tacit dimension" and builds his theoretical framework upon the observation that people can (and do) know more than they are able to express through language. In the remaining two chapters, the respective absence and presence of this dimension is explored in terms of the consequences for consciousness that follow.

CHAPTER IV

The Nature of Ordinary Consciousness

A Recapitulation

Although there are two modes of consciousness available most people experience only one, the ordinary consciousness of everyday life. But before discussing the major characteristics associated with this state of mind and the reasons for its predominance, it might do well to glance back over the ground covered thus far.

It was noted in the first chapter that educators have become increasingly aware that success and failure in school may have more to do with the values, judgments, and labels applied by school personnel than with the presumed inherent abilities of the students whom they process. The act of labeling itself, that is, of consistently identifying and responding to someone as "bright and promising" or "dull and lacking", seems to initiate a self-fulfilling spiral wherein situations become real largely because people define and act on them as real. When the world was called flat, for example, people behaved as though it was. And when a person or class of people is called "flat", that too seems to have the same effect of stymieing growth and limiting vision - for both parties involved.

Although some are becoming increasingly aware that this self-fulfilling process pervades the school system, most seem to be at a loss as to how to deal with it. In part, this reflects a paucity of theoretical models of knowledge capable of clarifying our understanding of labels as language symbols, and the role their meanings play in the way people come to know the world. What is also reflected here, however, is that people appear to have increasingly lost touch with a dormant or latent capability each person has to know the world free from the confines of labels; that is, to know the events of the world directly.

Thus, the second chapter offers a theoretical explanation of the role that language or labels play in the construction of our ways of knowing. From Mead and the symbolic interactionists one learns that labeling is both inevitable and indispensable to everyday life. People seem to be biogenetically "wired" for

41

this abstract activity and depend mightily on it for
a socially developed sense of both self and society.
So much so, in fact, that from the standpoint of the
sociology of knowledge one literally creates his social
realities by arriving at agreements or common definitions of "the way things are." Unfortunately, of course,
this leaves considerable room for error whereby worlds
and people are flattened by the names they are called.

Chapter three maintained that this propensity to
label is directly related to the active functions
associated with the left hemisphere of the brain, and
a cultural bias that favors a linear, lingual interpre-
tation of the meaning of occurring events. However, it
has also been discovered that this represents only
one of two major modes of knowing available and that
another, vastly different and yet complementary mode,
remains largely untapped in the right hemisphere. It
is this receptive-intuitive mode that holds the key to
knowing the world in some way other than through the
labeling intellect. The dilemma, however, springs
from the fact that people here are submerged in a culture which so worships reason, that most are unable to
even momentarily turn off the words in their heads and
see an object free from its labels. It is important
to emphasize that the potential to do so is inherent in
each person if one could but find a way of temporarily
quieting or putting to rest the momentum of the left
hemisphere. As it is, however, the major thrust of
this chapter on the nature of ordinary consciousness,
is to assert that it is filled (to the point of un-
healthy preoccupation) with words.

Ordinary Consciousness as a "Stream" - of Words

While it may initially sound contradictory to say
so, the broadest, most pervasive characteristic of consciousness appears to be movement; that is, fluidity
and change. William James (1890) maintained that no
mental state, once experienced, can ever be recaptured
in identical form. Whether one realizes it or not,
every sensation, every thought-movement, has a corre-
sponding cerebral action associated with it. The result is that one is always being modified in the process of interacting with the environment and for this
reason can never step back into the same experience
twice. "Experience is remolding us every moment, and
our mental reaction on any given thing is really a
resultant of our experience of the whole world up to

that date" (James, 1890). Theoretically, if not experientially then, interruptions in consciousness no more constitute breaks in it than do the joints in a piece of bamboo signal a break in the wood. As a result, James maintained that consciousness is more like a river or stream than a train or chain. It is flowing rather than jointed. "In talking of it hereafter," he said, "let us call it the stream of thought, of consciousness, or of subjective life." (1890)

Now while it is theoretically sound to postulate that consciousness is of an unbroken whole, individual self-consciousness is fragmented in that it is marked by a fundamental sense of separation from all else that exists in the world. This separation, interestingly, is something people both create and then attempt to bridge with words.

Although people are generally convinced that what they take in with their senses accurately represents what is "out there", those who study the matter are coming to agree that individualized or personal consciousness is extremely selective in nature and largely a compilation of socially created constructs, categories, definitions and expectations – all associated with a wide variety of situations. Language cojoles and coerces one into believing that it represents the last word in knowing. Instead, however, it makes still-life out of moving, living, patterned relationships and thus robs human being of its vitality which is change. At the center of this labeling process, and the most powerful social construct of all, is the very sense of self every individual holds and through which he or she learns to approach and negotiate the world.

Ordinary Consciousness as Self-Consciousness

Through the social psychology of George Herbert Mead it was revealed that the most distinguishing feature of the self is its relationship to itself as an object. One is not only conscious, but also self-conscious. People are aware of their awareness and know that they know. They listen to themselves as they talk and relate to others, and then adjust their behavior on the basis of their perceptions of the way significant others are going to respond to their words or actions. It is this reflexive nature of consciousness, this ability of the human subject to alternately engage itself as an object, that is the most distin-

guishing characteristic of selfhood. This self-reflex-
ive capacity, with its roots deeply imbedded in the
central nervous system, only manifests as self-consciousness in the presence of language and meaning. It
is the word or label as vocal gesture, then, which gives
rise to the self; to the sense of "I-ness."

    This point is essential to a full understanding of
the extent to which the labeling process is involved in
one's very being, and why it is consequently so difficult for people to free themselves from its influence.
Language is the vehicle through which people come into
existence as social selves and then depend on it,
through the remainder of their lives, for a sense of
meaning, purpose, and difference with regard to everything else that is. For people come to know themselves
in the reverberation of their own words; in the echo of
their meanings and the responses they elicit from others.
Most humans make their way through the world in this
manner never thinking there could be any other way of
knowing; never knowing without first having to think.

    The following comments from Helen Keller clearly
express the immense significance of the role that language plays in human consciousness. She illustrates
beautifully the way in which labels create the "things"
of the world which in turn comprise our "realities."

                    We walked down the path to the
                    wellhouse, attracted by the fra-
                    grance of the honeysuckle with
                    which it was covered. Someone
                    was drawing water and my teacher
                    placed my hand under the spout.
                    As the cool stream gushed over my
                    hand she spelled into the other
                    the word water, first slowly,
                    then rapidly. I stood still, my
                    whole attention fixed upon the
                    motion of her fingers. Suddenly
                    I felt a misty consciousness as of
                    something forgotten - a thrill of
                    returning thought; and somehow the
                    mystery of language was revealed to
                    me, I knew that W-A-T-E-R meant
                    that wonderful cool something that
                    was flowing over my hand. That
                    living word awakened my soul, gave
                    it light, hope, joy, set it free!
                    There were barriers still, it is

44

true, but barriers that in time
could be swept away.

I left the well house eager to
learn. Everything had a name,
and each name gave birth to a
new thought. As we returned
into the house, every object
which I touched seemed to quiver
with life. That was because I
saw everything with the strange,
new sight that had come to me
(in Sagan, 1977).

In much the same way, society creates the social
self of the individual, primarily through the institu-
tion of the family and the process of socialization.
Once one is born one is taught his or her name, the
appropriate sex-role behavior this name should exhibit,
and that, for example, one has a body, dreams, goals,
fears, and a whole host of other things. Through
words, then, a dichotomous line is created; on one
side of which I am, while on the other there is all
else.

It is from within this dualistic frame of reference that people look out upon and label the "things"
of the world.

Self-Consciousness and The Illusion of Separation

People have come to rely so heavily on the left
hemispheric activity of labeling and defining that our
culture generally assumes it to be synonomous with
understanding. Moreover, words have allowed people to
define themselves and to label what they consider to be
a particular segment of their experience as "I".

William James (1890) noted that ". . . the elementary psychic fact is not thought or this thought or
that thought, but my thought, every thought being
owned." The sense of "I-ness" is a universal fact of
ordinary consciousness. It is the seat of experience
from which one looks out, labels, and judges the world.
It is an experience so profoundly real to everyone that
the suggestion "it" may be an illusion created and
foist upon us through societal convention, generally
draws expressions of incredulity. How could the very
foundation of our sense of being-in-the-world be
illusory, one asks? How could "I" not be real?

45

Nevertheless, it is precisely this notion of the existence of a separate self that people must come to see through if they are ever to learn to approach one another free from the preconceptions created by the labeling process. It is largely because people think and feel themselves to be cut off and separated from everyone (or thing) else that they are so quick to label and categorize. When people consider themselves to be absolutely apart from one another with no ties or connections, what possible stake could one have in the being of another?

If one fundamentally thinks and feels himself to be as an island unto himself, then it is difficult to be concerned with anything but the welfare of one's own piece of real estate. However, the sensation and assumption of the existence of a separate "I", a personal entity considered to be the "real me" and encased somewhere deep within the headbrain, may be a socially created illusion of sorts, a dramatically erroneous misconception of the nature of the self that carries with it social consequences of immense proportion. A closer look at the dynamics involved in the creation of this myth of the separate self should establish the point more clearly.

Most people, it seems, when given the opportunity to reflect on what they consider to be the essence of themselves, conceive of this essence as an inner-abiding entity. One typically assigns a location to this entity experiencing "it" as residing somewhere behind the eyes and between the ears. There is a tendency to think and feel that the real me is a separate entity unto itself, locked up inside the head, and from which point the rest of the body is suspended. The running dialog that goes on in the head as one talks things over with one's self appears to be absolute proof of the existence, location, and thus reality of this inner-abiding "me". There must be an engineer at the wheel, it is reasoned, there must be something.

The self-consciousness of everyday life, then, sees itself as a skin-ensconsed entity residing somewhere behind one's eyes such that "I" and "my eyes" are considered to be two separate phenomena. At the root of this sensation are two related processes: the social convention of a language structure, and memory.

The self-conscious experience is typically turned

46

inward through the coercive structure of a language which defines situations and experience as happening to me. People are told that they have experience and not, for example, that they are them. Some of these are defined for the individual as experiences "I" am desirous of, while others represent ones "I" do not want to have, "You don't want to hurt yourself," we are informed. Or we are instructed, "You want to make a good impression now, don't you?" And this, it must be emphasized, is how the misconception is perpetrated! R. D. Laing (1967) calls this societally induced confusion the "mystification of experience" reflecting an enormous capacity humans have for deceiving themselves and then taking their own lies for truth.

> By such mystification, we achieve and sustain our adjustment, adaptation, socialization. But the result of such adjustment to our society is that, having been tricked and having tricked outselves out of our minds, that is to say, out of our own personal worlds of experience, out of that unique meaning with which potentially we may endow the external world, simultaneously we have been conned into the illusion that we are separate 'skin-encapsuled egos.' Having at one and the same time lost our selves and developed the illusion that we are autonomous egos, we are expected to comply by inner consent with external constraints, to an almost unbelievable extent (Laing, 1967).

The concept of socialization refers to the transmission of society's norms, values, and expectations to societal newcomers; learning the rules of a variety of social "games", if you will. But as it manifests itself in the interaction setting it is not made clear that these are society's wants and desires. Rather, one is led to believe by parents, teachers, friends, relatives and just about everyone else, that they are one's own. Other people essentially teach individuals who they are and what they want. In fact, it is precisely because people are both in and of society, rather then separate and apart from it, that they are able to be hoodwinked so thoroughly into believing that there is a fixed and permanent inner core called

"I".

Recall, however, that the power of Mead's work came from his having established both mind and self to be social creations and therefore not bounded by the skin of an individual. Instead, he maintained that any given individual self ". . . must extend as far as the social activity or apparatus of social relations which constitutes it extends; and hence that field cannot be bounded by the skin of the individual organism to which it belongs" (Mead, 1934). But, alas, people are not awake to this fact of their existence: that society is an extension of one's self, and one's self an expression of it. Human beings are really much more than they credit themselves as being. They are the social field out of which they arise but have virtually no notion, let alone experience, of this in the reality of their everyday lives.

If one is not convinced by parents, peers, and practically everyone else that the "real you" is locked inside one's body, there is the mixed blessing of memory to put the finishing touches on the illusion being created. It is memory that contributes to the sensation of constancy, of being the same I one was moments, months, or millenia ago. It creates the impression that outside events are changing at a much faster rate than this consistent inside sense of one's self, and thus sustains the sensation of an independent I who observes the passing procession of life. The work of the philosopher Allen Watts has shed considerable light on this matter. He asserts:

> If you imagine that memory is a
> direct knowledge of the past
> rather than a present experience,
> you get the illusion of knowing
> the past and the present at the
> same time. This suggests that
> there is something in you distinct
> from both the past and the present
> experience, and it is different
> from the past experience. If I
> can compare the two, and notice that
> experience has changed, I must be
> something constant and apart
> (Watts, 1951).

If the matter is carefully examined, it is appar-

ent that one cannot actually compare a present experience with any past experience. All that can be done
is to compare it with a memory of the past. And this
recollection of the past is really an experience occurring in the present! Once it is fully realized that
memory is actually a present-centered experience, it
becomes increasingly clear that there is no one existing separate and apart from this experience. Just as
there is simply thinking that occurs and not someone
thinking thoughts, so there is just experience and not
someone experienceing experience. Though one may
search painstakingly, no one can find an "I" which
exists apart from a present consciousness experience.
They are, instead, one and the same.

There is an ancient Chinese tale worth recounting
here that makes the point succinctly. It seems that
a young aspirant on the path to self-realization
approached a great master saying, "I am without peace
of mind. Put my mind at rest for me please." The
master responded, "Bring out your mind (i.e., your 'I')
and I will pacify it for you." To this the aspirant
replied, "Though I have sought my mind for years and
years I have been unable to find it." "There," pro-
claimed the sage, "it is pacified!"

The mystic Rajneesh (1976) makes precisely the
same point in identifying the common misconception of
mind-as-an-entity as the "root problem of all problems."

> If you watch, you will never come
> across an entity like mind. It
> is not a thing it is just a process;
> it is not a thing, it is like a
> crowd. Individual thoughts exist,
> but they move so fast that you cannot
> see the gaps in between. The inter-
> vals cannot be seen because you are
> not very aware and alert, you need
> a deeper insight. When your eyes can
> look deep, you will suddenly see one
> thought, another thought, another
> thought - but no mind.
>
> Thoughts together, millions of
> thoughts, give you the illusion that
> mind exists. It is just like a crowd,
> millions of people standing in a
> crowd: is there any such thing as a
> crowd? Can you find the crowd apart

49

from the individuals standing
there? But they are standing
together and their togetherness
gives you the feeling that something like a crowd exists - only
individuals exist. . . . Watch,
and you will find thoughts, but you
will never come across the mind
(Rajneesh, 1976).

Ordinary Consciousness: In Need of a Change

It is the nature of ordinary consciousness to be
in constant motion. This movement is perpetuated by
a stream of words and thought-forms which are generated
by the activity of the surrounding social order and
subsequently internalized by the emerging individual.
The most powerful and consequential of these internalized social constructs is the sense people come to have
of their "real selves" as independent ego-agents separated from and imprisoned within their bodies. It is
this sense of separation, it has been argued, that
makes it relatively easy for people to judge and label
everything and everyone they encounter, especially
those whom are discovered to be distressingly different. The I with which people are identified, the I of
"I-want" and "I-have", is more of an idea than an
entity. It is perhaps the most pervasive and powerful
idea on the face of the earth and is the very foundation upon which all relationships are built, maintained and destroyed. But if people are even to entertain
the notion of engaging one another free from the dis-
colorations created by labels, then this common,
everyday sense of the self as separate and estranged
must change.

This process of what can be called the "separation
of the self" is initiated in the family, and then reinforced and sustained in the school system. Schools
are progressively organized around the generalized
notion that competition amongst these separate selves
eventually keeps separate the chaff from the wheat -
labor from professions, the blue from the white collar
workers. But the process of labeling, it has been
noted, goes a long way toward creating and maintaining
the chaff and wheat distinctions the schools so ardu-
ously endeavor to identify! Moreover, by so labeling
and categorizing, they encourage the acceptance of a
mechanical model of man and his relationships that is

static and rigid with its implication that people really are what they are labeled - that one inherently is a "slow learner", "troublemaker", "brain", "bad apple", "C student", or what have your,

When people view one another in this way, they are prevented from realizing selfhood as capable of being anything more than what is allowed by the language used to describe it. Labels are rigid, they freeze reality into categorical cubes which do not allow for elasticity and growth. The following passage from Aldous Huxley's The Doors of Perception (1954), states the case most eloquently,

> Every individual is at once the beneficiary and the victim of the linguistic tradition into which he has been born - the beneficiary inasmuch as language gives access to the accumulated record of other people's experience, the victim in so far as it confirms him in the belief that reduced awareness is the only awareness and as it bedevils his sense of reality, so that he is all to apt to take his concepts for data, his words for actual things.

Ordinary consciousness is consciousness as experienced through the interpretive filter of a language. It is consciousness broken up by a grid-work of definitions and meanings accentuated by a powerful sense of oneself as an entity, separate and apart from the things being defined,

But it is known, now, that this represents only one of two available modes of seeing the world and one's relationship within it, There is another more holistic-intuitive experience to be had which reveals a common ground of Being that all people share through their humanity. Another perspective with an entirely different angle of vision is available which opens into a realm of consciousness that is "non-ordinary" indeed. This is a point of view of the world where differences are dissolved in a fundamental unity which emerges as an underlying principle of cohesiveness integrating all things, Linked to the capacity of the right hemisphere to induce holistic mentation, this is the perfect complementary countermeasure to the tendency to fragment the flow of the world with words.

Before discussing the characteristics of non-ordinary consciousness in the following chapter, it must be made clear that something more is involved in the processes of mind and consciousness than mere alterations in brain functioning. It is this "something more" that allows one to speak, if only metaphorically, of distinct spheres or realms of consciousness. Roger Sperry has drawn such a conclusion from his extensive neuro-surgical research. "Although inseparably tied to the material brain process, it (consciousness) is something distinct and special in its own right, 'different from and more than' its component physiochemical elements" (Sperry, in Annual Editions, 1978).

In a similar vein the neuro-surgeon Wilder Penfield (1975) asserts that, after years of study and research, he was brought to the conclusion that the reflex action of the brain cannot account for the phenomenon of awareness or consciousness. They are two related but distinctly different forms of energy. To illustrate this, Penfield points to the experience of a patient who has had an electrode strategically placed in the interpretive cortex. Suddenly an experience from the past is vividly recalled and the patient's consciousness is doubled. He is simultaneously aware of what is occurring in the operating room and the "flashback" from the past. What is more, he is able to clearly discuss the meaning of both thought-streams.

> The patient's mind, which is considering the situation in such an aloof and critical manner, can only be something quite apart from neuronal reflex action. It is noteworthy that two streams of consciousness are flowing, the one driven by input from the environment, the other by an electrode delivering sixty pulses per second to the cortex. The fact that there should be no confusion in the conscious state suggests that, although the content of consciousness depends in large measure on neuronal activity, awareness itself does not. (Penfield, 1975).

52

This, indeed, is the point to be underscored. There is a distinct and significant difference between the contents of consciousness and consciousness in and of itself. To be identified with the contents of consciousness, as most people are, is to largely restrict one's identity and world-of-meaning to that which society has imposed. It is only through the transcendence of these societal impositions that mind moves from ordinary to non-ordinary awareness.

CHAPTER V

The Nature of Non-Ordinary Consciousness

The Need for a New Image of Man

We have been saying that the most poignant characteristics of ordinary consciousness are the sense of self-conscious separation associated with the feeling of I-ness, and an over.dependence upon language and labels to provide meaning in life. It has been suggested that the idea and sensation of one's self as an isolated particle stems both from memory, and the interpersonal dynamics of having been labeled as such throughout the process of socialization. Needless to say, this contributes significantly to our predilection to chop the world up into bits and pieces with words. People label everything, themselves, other people, other groups, other nations - everything.

This activity of the intellect, associated with the action-mode of the left cerebral hemisphere, is so predominant in this society (and most others, for that matter) that one cannot help but wonder if such overspecialization might not ultimately threaten the adaptive capacity of the species. Locked into the notion of separateness, people are inclined to treat others in ways that promote suffering for all involved. In fact, it is predominantly this sense of separateness that has allowed for the extensive pollution of the ecosystem - so immersed are people in the illusion that they are unconnected to anybody or anything.

The analytic activity of the left hemisphere carries with it the ability to isolate or separate the various events of the world. This capacity for discrimination had tremendous survival value for the species in the struggle to gain dominion over what was perceived to be a hostile environment. However, times have changed; and the need to divide and conquer one's surroundings is not nearly as great as the need to complement and cooperate. Nearly ten years ago in the New York Post, U-Thant announced:

> I do not wish to seem overdramatic,
> but I can only conclude from the
> information that is available to me
> as Secretary General of the United
> Nations that the members of the

United Nations have perhaps 10
years left in which to subordinate
their ancient quarrels and launch
a global partnership to end the
arms race, to improve the human
environment, to defuse the population explosion, and to supply the
required momentum to world development efforts. If such a global partnership is not forged within the next
decade, then I very much fear that
the problems I have mentioned will
have reached such staggering propor-
tions that they will be beyond our
capacity to control (New York Post,
May 15, 1969, p.47)

That was almost a decade ago and very little, if
anything, has changed in the interim. The problems of
today are international, global problems that demand
tremendous cooperative efforts for their resolution.
In the absence of such cooperation all mankind stands
to lose. There is dramatic need of a new concept of
man and the nature of his relationship with the people
and processes of his world.

If people are ever to change behavior that is increasingly recognized as self-defeating, they must
first perceive that there is some alternative way of
being available. In other words, there must first be
a change in the way people view their relationship to
one another and their environment.

The seeds of just such a revised image are inherent in the knowledge that each human being has the right
hemispheric capacity to experience the world in a radically different, yet complementary way. Just as the
left hemisphere allows one to isolate and identify what
appear to be the segments or parts of an overall process, so the right can provide a direct intuitive grasp
of the patterned relationships comprising the whole.
In the first instance there is something akin to notic-
ing the trees - each one at a time. While in the
second, one comes upon the forest as though from on
high and can see its nature - its simultaneous shape,
size, and juxtaposition to houses, highways or what
have you.

The Complementary Nature of the Two Perspectives

The principle of complementarity explains that each of these perspectives yields a view of the reality of trees that may be correct - but not complete. This is what is being proposed here. The point is not to argue for the exclusive adoption of the intuitive over the intellectual mode of perception, but rather to reinforce the notion that there are two distinctively different ways of apprehending the world available. The decision as to which mode of perception to employ would depend upon what it was one wanted to know, and then having the ability to apply either or both modes of knowing.

It may be helpful to return for a moment to the analogy of the tree and the forest to establish this point more clearly. In the event, for example, that one was interested in diagnosing and treating a part-icularly voracious deciduous disease, it would be essential to examine the infected trees - one by one if necessary. But if on another occasion a stand of timber was endangered by a sudden fire, one would need to see the blaze in relation to the forest as a whole. In this case, to become preoccupied with any of the trees individually would be to invite certain disaster.

The problems threatening the peoples of the world today are primarily of the nature of forest fires. They require the inclusion of a gestaltian view from above if they are to be fully understood and worked out.

This is an age where the radioactive dust from a nuclear test-explosion in China can fall across the midwestern United States and affect everything from the quality of the air, to the price of produce. This is an age where the facts of man's biological and ecological interdependence are becoming more apparent. It has become increasingly difficult to believe that national and geographic boundaries are real, and that they actually keep separate the people and problems of the world. All around there is growing evidence to support the idea that the earth and its "things" are inextricably interwoven in one unified bio-system that must ultimately be expanded to include being integrated in a solar system, a galaxy, and the universe at large (LeShan, 1966).

The quality of mind that perceives this underlying integration comes more from the intuitive than the intellectual side of the self. The problem is largely one of ignorance. People have ignored the intuitive side of themselves to such an extent that most are not aware that it exists; and of those who are, fewer still are able to call upon this mode of perception at will. Nevertheless, it does exist and is available to those who are willing to take the time to find and practice various techniques which will encourage its emergence. As Rollo May (1953) pointed out, "man does not grow automatically like a tree, but fulfills his potentialities only as he in his own consciousness plans and chooses." Choosing to shed the cultural "blinders" obscuring one's vision is not an easy task, however. The mind has been conditioned since birth to think and respond in routinized patterns that have become quite automatic.

The Automatization of Mind

Ordinary consciousness, it has been shown, is largely a social-personal construction. The act of thinking is fundamentally a reactive process of habituation to socially constructed thought-forms and meanings. Through repeated exposure to what appears to be the same events occurring over and over again, people come to expect the same sounds, sights, tastes and aromas to be forever associated with what become the familiar things of one's world. Noises from the highway are absorbed as "cars", movements across the street immediately become "the neighbors", commotion from upstairs is understood as "the kids", and the human being who comes home from work each night is experienced as "my husband" or "the wife." It is this process of habituation and desensitization to the fluid becoming of the universe that led Jerome Bruner and his colleagues (1957) to the conclusion that what people really experience are not the actual events of the physical world, but rather the mental categories they have come to associate with these events. In a similar vein, Hastorf and Cantrill (1954) concluded that "the significances assumed by different happenings for different people depend in large part on the purposes people bring to the occasion and the assumptions they have of the purposes and probable behavior of other people involved." And in reviewing the results of a variety of research experiments in perception, Ittelson and Kilpatric (1967) maintained;

. . . that perception is never a
sure thing, never an absolute
revelation of 'what is.' Rather,
what we see is a prediction - our
own personal construction designed
to give us the best possible bet
for carrying out our purposes in
action. We make these bets on the
basis of our past experience.

In the context of the classroom setting, then, the
teacher never really sees Johnny but a series of ideas
about him instead. And, in the case of the classic
bigot, it is never the living, breathing other that is
acknowledged - only the emotionally charged stereotypic
constructs set off in the mind as a stimulus-response.
This is why it is essential to learn to by-pass the
languaging side of mind if one is to experience some
interlude of escape from the constraints imposed by the
labeling process. In the following passage from the
linguist Benjamin Lee Whorf, the incredible power of
language to construct the contents of consciousness is
made abundantly clear.

Actually, thinking is most mysterious,
by far the greatest light upon it that
we have is thrown by the study of language. This study shows that the forms
of a person's thoughts are controlled
by the inexorable laws of pattern of
which he is unconscious. These patterns are the unperceived intricate
systemizations of his own language -
his thinking itself is in a language -
and every language is a vast pattern-
system, different from others, in which
are culturally ordained the forms and
categories by which the personality
not only communicates, but also analyzes
nature, notices or neglects types of
relationships and phenomena, channels
his reasoning, and builds the house
of his consciousness (Whorf, in Carroll,
1956).

The Deautomatization of Mind

Freeing one's self from this "house" that language
has built is a matter of acting upon the realization

59

that that which has been constructed can be re-construct-
ed. For it is not as though the words are neural path-
ways of the brain so that in clearing consciousness of
language some essential part of the anatomy is removed.
The brain is the primary biological mechanism in humans
through which consciousness is made manifest, but they
are not one and the same phenomenon. Sir Charles
Sherrington, the British physiologist considered by
some to be the most esteemed life scientist of this
century, spent a lifetime studying the brain. He concluded that the human mind could not be reduced to
physical energy nor understood through related constructs and was, therefore, essentially free of those
constraints. "The two for all I can do remain refrac-
torily apart. They seem to me disparate; not mutually
convertible; untranslatable the one into the other"
(in Matson, 1966).

The key that unlocks the doors of perception lies
buried in the intricacies of the neglected right hemisphere. It is through this cerebral avenue that one
may be ushered into a totally different dimension of
consciousness: a dimension characterized by unity and
oneness rather than diversity and separation. Getting
there, however, requires undergoing what Arthur Deikman
(1966) has called a process of deautomatization: a procedure whereby the actions and percepts of the routinized, taken-for-granted-world of consciousness are re-
invested with a focused attention that is usually dis-
sipated in conceptualization about the world.

Before exploring a particular technique of deautomatization it is important to point out that this
phenomenon has been found to be associated with a wide
variety of activities, both intentional and spontaneous
in nature. For example, submersion in a sensory de-
privation tank and so called alpha machines which feed
back information indicating the brain is producing
alpha waves associated with right hemispheric activity,
are illustrations of actions specifically undertaken to
by-pass the intellectualizing component of mind. Similarly, hallucinogenic drugs like mescaline, LSD, peyote
and marihuana, and various techniques of concentration
and meditation, can also function to take one into
various spheres and levels of the intuitive realm of
consciousness and the experiences to be had therein.
But these experiences are not reserved for mystics,
"acid heads", or those who pursue the occult. They can
and do occur spontaneously to all kinds of people and

60

are triggered by a wide variety of situations. In a
book entitled Ecstacy: A Way of Knowing (1974),
Andrew M. Greeley describes a wide range of ecstatic
experiences which can occur.

> A man looking up at a star-filled sky
> loses himself for hours in the depths
> of the universe. A mother feels peace
> and joy surge over her as she watches
> over her sleeping baby. A troubled
> young student, full of doubt and fears,
> suddenly finds his anxieties dispelled
> as an inexpressible feeling takes posses-
> sion of him. Each of these people has
> experienced an interlude of mystical
> ecstacy.

The fact that these mystical interludes can occur
as spontaneously as they do simply suggests that the
capacity for this experience is inherent in the human
organism as such. But if one's interest lies in con-
ciously cultivating the ability to shift from one mode
of perception to the other, it is necessary to develop
techniques designed to do just that. Moreover, if a
society becomes interested in making this an integrated
part of a school curriculum, then the simplest and least
expensive method would, at least initially, be most ad-
antageous.

Thought Watching: A Technique of Deautomatization

To see the world in some way other than through
words, labels, and categories requires that some way
of turning off that activity of the mind be implemented.
The technique to be outlined here is a form of <u>thought
watching</u>, of directed attention to the movement of the
mind, and thus is associated with a meditative-contem-
lative approach which has been used to quiet the dis-
cursive mind for thousands of years. It is relatively
simple and, with continued practice, very effective
which is why it is offered here as an illustrative
technique. It is based on the principle that consciousness and the <u>contents</u> of consciousness are two different
phenomena, much in the same way that a movie screen and
that which is projected upon the screen also differ.
By and large, the content of consciousness is social.
It is made up of the labels, categories, and definitions
of situations from which, it has been contended, realities are constructed. This is what must be cleansed

from the screen of consciousness if one is to have a new and different vision of the world.

Roberto Assagioli (1971) describes the need for such a psychological cleansing as a necessary first step in preparing the mind for the reception of intuitive insight.

> The first step is of a negative character - the temporary checking or elimination from the field of consciousness of other functions which generally have a spontaneous and uninterrupted activity. Constantly, sensations from the outer world or from the body intrude into the field of consciousness and makes either the entrance or the recognition of intuitions impossible or difficult. Therefore, it is necessary to carry out what we might call a psychological cleaning of the field of consciousness; metaphorically, to insure that the projection screen is clear and white. This permits in the subject a sympathetic opening of the consciousness towards, or a reaching actively for, that truth or section of reality with which he seeks to come into contact for the solution of a human or an impersonal cognition problem.

The key to thought watching as a technique for cleansing consciousness lies in the focusing of attention on the contents of consciousness. For when consciousness or, as the Buddhists refer to it, "mindfulness" folds back upon itself and watches its own movement dispassionately and without attachment, a two-stage process of deautomatization occurs.

The first is that the meaning and sense of one's conceptualizations about the taken-for-granted-world become much less taken for granted. One comes to see with unusual clarity that labels are merely abstractions that always, with varying degrees of accuracy, refer to a more profound reality beyond themselves. The second stage, about which there will be more to say later, is

62

a state of "no-mind" where the screen of consciousness is undisturbed by thought forms and is potentially commensurate with what has come to be identified as the entire "field of consciousness" (Baba, 1975).

Consciousness can be freed from the influences of labels by learning to look and see with both unwavering perseverance and dispassionate detachment. Allan Watts describes the process clearly:

> That is to say, one begins to take an objective view of the stream of thoughts, impressions, feelings, and experiences which constantly flows through the mind. Instead of trying to control and interfere with it, one simply lets it flow as it pleases. But whereas consciousness normally lets itself be carried away by the flow, in this case the important thing is to <u>watch</u> the flow without being carried away . . . one simply accepts experiences as they come without interfering with them on the one hand or identifying oneself with them on the other. One does not judge them, form theories about them, try to control them, or attempt to change their nature in any way; one lets them be free to be just exactly what they are. 'The perfect man,' said Chuang-tzu, 'employs his mind as a mirror; it grasps nothing, it refuses nothing, it receives but does not keep.' This must be quite clearly distinguished from mere empty-mindedness on the one hand, and from ordinary undisciplined mind wandering on the other (quoted by Naranjo, in Ornstein 1973).

When one learns to reinvest actual behavior or intellectual constructs with a focused attention, an attention that is typically expended in abstract con-ceptualization <u>about</u> these aspects of everyday life, the nature of knowledge undergoes a remarkable change from knowing about - to directly knowing <u>of</u> the thing, event or problem under investigation. Th<u>is</u> is the sense in which this knowledge is said to be transcen-dental. It stands over-against the socio-cultural definitions constructing the meaning of situations and so frees one from knowing through these interpretive constraints.

Abraham Maslow has described a very similar state of mind as being characteristic of those who encounter "peak experiences." Here a kind of knowledge occurs that Maslow calls "B cognition":

> In the peak experience, we become more detached, more objective, and we are more able to perceive the world as if it were independent not only of the perceiver but even of human beings in general. The perceiver can more readily look upon nature as if it were there in itself and for itself, not simply as if it were a human playground put there for human purposes. He can more easily refrain from projecting human purposes upon it. In a word, he can see it in its own Being (as an end in itself) rather than as something to be used or something to be afraid of or something to wish for or to be reacted to in some other personal, human, self-centered way (Maslow, in Greeley, 1974).

By disengaging one's self and examining the taken-for-granted meaning structures defining the "realities" of a given situation, a process of deautomatization is initiated and accompanied by a shift from left to right hemispheric perceiving. Once such a perceptual shift is accomplished, the foundation is laid for a change in one's behavioral approach to the world. For if the world is truly perceived differently, people are much more likely to begin to behave differently. This is why the inclusion of intuitive instruction in the schools is considered here to be so essential to the holistic growth of the individual.

This deautomatized perceptual shift is encouraged and developed as one increasingly adjusts the locus of self-identification from actions, thoughts, and emotions, to a witnessing center of being which observes the dramatic play of life from an unaffected distance. It is this distancing phenomenon that creates the space

64

so essential to the expansion of awareness.

By establishing the distance and detachment necessary to witness the nature of one's involvements in
the world, a unique mode of "seeing" is acquired that
is free from emotional entanglement. In this way, the
taken-for-granted thoughts, feelings, and behaviors
which structure one's life are seen for what they are;
programs that have been run through the mind so ex-
tensively that they now manifest as habitual re-runs.
Without this distance, one is simply too close to see -
unable to see the forest for the trees. In such a
state of awareness one's identity is increasingly associated with this witnessing state of being and not
with that which is being witnessed. This transference
of identity frees one from psychological attachment
to previously unexamined societal scripts and represents a distinct educative awakening, the likes of
which rarely occur in traditional academic settings.

In an interview with Sam Keen (1970), the established neurophysiologist-biophysicist John Lilly discussed some of the consequences of establishing the
witnessing self.

> As soon as you get distance you
> realize you are not the programmer,
> and you are not that which is pro-
> grammed, and you are not the program.
> Your identity becomes established as
> an independent agent. Once this
> ability to disidentify yourself from
> old programs, programming, and from
> the programmer becomes generalized,
> you have the key to higher states
> of consciousness (Lilly, in Keen, 1970).

Regardless of the technique used, deautomatization
brings about a release from the verbal chains that
bind self-consciousness. When this occurs, one comes
into the boundless "field of consciousness" where the
quality and depth of experience range from an indes-
cribable peace and joy as a mother watches over her
sleeping child, to a complete absorption in the identi-
fication with the Creative Principle or Godhead of the
universe as in "I and my father are one."

The "Field" of Consciousness: An Organizing Principle

To come to some understanding of what is usually

defined as the expansion of awareness associated with intuitive insight, it is important to clearly distinguish between consciousness and self consciousness - between consciousness on the one hand, and its contents on the other.

In a superb article entitled "The Meaning of Everything," Arthur Deikman (in Ornstein, 1973) has essentially summarized the position of Eastern metaphysics regarding the relationship of individual self-consciousness to a broader, universal "field" of awareness.

According to this perspective, human beings are inextricably enmeshed in a gigantic biosystem that incorporates both the organic and inorganic systems of the universe. This system is organized on two fundamental and complementary levels which extend throughout the universe: the biological and the psychological. At the biological level this organization manifests as life, while at the psychological level it is expressed as awareness or consciousness. Awareness tends to be experienced as localized (as my awareness or your awareness) because people confuse consciousness, which extends equally throughout the universe, with the thought-contents of consciousness which are localized through the sensory-cognitive systems of the individual and thus help create the separate sense of I.

Deikman suggests that one try a simple experiment as a means of realizing this important difference. He proposes that:

> (o)ur visual activity is usually experienced as being identical with awareness. However, if you close your eyes, you will recognize that your awareness and your visual field are not the same. Try it now. Once again, close your eyes and ask yourself what constitutes your awareness. With your eyes closed, you will tend to identify awareness with sounds and body sensations. If next you imagine these sounds and sensations to be absent, you will appreciate the fact that awareness is something other than sensations or thoughts (in Ornstein, 1973).

Eastern metaphysicians like to compare the inte-grated biosystem of the individual and the universe with a pond. When the system is at rest, that is, not engaged in the localized activity of thought formation, it is clear, serene, and perfectly reflective: it is not doing or becoming - it simply is. Again, the tan-tric master Rajneesh (1976) describes the situation with an eloquent simplicity that only seems to come from direct experience.

> The innermost being is just like a
> mirror. Whatsoever comes before it,
> it mirrors, it simply becomes a
> witness. Disease comes or health,
> hunger or satiety, summer or winter,
> childhood or old age, birth or death -
> whatsoever happens happens before the
> mirror, it never happens to the
> mirror . . . . Your inner sky never
> becomes anything - it is a being, it
> never becomes anything. All becoming
> is just getting identified with some
> form and name, some colour, some form
> arising in space - all becoming. You
> are a being, you are already that - no
> need to become anything (Rajneesh, 1976).

When, through whatever set of circumstances, one comes to be established in this state of awareness, the occurrence is typically experienced as being wonder-fully expansive and liberating, the result of having been temporarily freed from the delimiting and restric-tive sensation of ego or "I-ness." This is generally accompanied by a very powerful and overwhelming sense of unity and oneness, an emerging sense that one actu-ally is the pattern of integration and wholeness being experienced. This is a state of pure awareness and perfect relationship complete unto itself. It is com-plete because it is one, there being no "ego-I" to create the world and its manifold things.

However, once the localized activity of thought formulation is initiated, it represents a disturbance at the surface of the water, like so many stones being tossed into it. It is this disturbance of the reflec-tive quality of the pond that prevents people from identifying their consciousness as that which pervades the universe. Less metaphorically, of course, this disturbance represents the words and labels of a language system expressed in the beliefs and assumptions that define one's realities, Most people spend most of their lives within this comparatively tiny sphere of awareness,

Consciousness pervades the universe, but self-consciousness or the knowledge of one's own consciousness only occurs in those organisms designed to allow for this, Only in the "man-body", it is said, can a living organism come to know its true nature or real self - which is an inherent oneness with all that is (Singh, 1977), It is not surprising, then, that those who enter the field-of-consciousness experience with any degree of intensity generally find that it re-organizes, revitalizes, and ultimately revolutionizes their lives.

Common Characteristics of the "Field Experience"

There are several characteristics commonly associated with the fuller expressions of this field experience; among them are, egolessness, unity, ineffability, and a profound sensation of the realness of what has occurred, Given that the experience can vary in intensity, duration, and frequency depending to some extent upon what, if anything, is being done to induce it, it follows that not all of the characteristics necessarily manifest for every person in every instance.

Nevertheless, those to be discussed here have been reported with such consistency throughout the ages, that they must be included in a general discussion of the nature of non-ordinary reality. Moreover, they help to clarify the sense in which "field" consciousness can remedy the ego-centered condition of being-in-the-world by presenting a very different, experiential view of reality.

Inherent in the process of deautomatization, is a withering or dropping away of the common ego or "I" sensation as the center of existence from and to which everything else either goes or comes (Watts, 1961, 1966). This is the I that desires, that wants what it perceives to be other than itself. This is the familiar I that sees itself as a separate, skin enclosed entity apart from and in competition with others for a whole host of things, This is the I of ordinary consicousness that knows itself and others only through labels,

One of Greeley's subjects recounts a spontaneous and isolated experience occurring when he was a young boy of fifteen:

> Suddenly, and without warning, some-
> thing invisible seemed to be drawn
> across the sky, transforming the
> world about me into a kind of tent
> of concentrated and enhanced signifi-
> cance. What had been merely an out-
> side became an inside. The objective
> was somehow transformed into a
> completely subjective fact, which
> was experienced as 'mine,' but on a
> level where the word had no meaning;
> for 'I' was no longer the familiar
> ego (Greeley, 1974).

Rollo May (1953) pointed out that there is indeed a kind of self-forgetting that occurs on what he called a fourth level of consciousness. "But the word self-forgetting is a poor term; this consciousness in another sense is the most fulfilled state of human existence." This fulfillment is derived from the sensation of expansive integration which pervades the entire experience.

In place of the familiar ego sensation of separation there grows instead a feeling of oneness and unity - that one is the wholeness that is happening and that everything is unfolding just as it should be. This "I" is an expression of "I exist" rather than "I desire", of being rather than becoming, and is completely integrated with the perfect state of relationship that is perceived as pervading all things. This is the manner in which "one comes to see the self in all things, and all things in the self." This helps to understand the mystic's claim to be "one with the universe," or his assertion that "Nature (or God) manifests Itself as man, so that It might come to know Itself." Here, one is simply reminded that no other animal but man appears to have either the capacity or potential to be aware of the full nature of its own existence to the extent that humans do.

Regardless of all the words written about this experience, from the simplest to the most eloquent, in the final analysis it is invariably considered to be ineffable, and nothing, of course, makes better sense.

How could words possibly hope to describe a realm of experience which by definition passes beyond language before it is initiated? It must be remembered that this experience is triggered by the coming into prominence of right hemispheric functions, functions that are not associated with language and its definitions and meanings. The result is that one may be left with an experience, perhaps more real than anything ever experienced before, and yet be unable to find words that adequately convey even a semblance of the scope, depth, and power of the vision one has been privy to - if only for a moment. Nevertheless, the existing literature in the area, particularly from those who offer evidence of being established in this state of mind at will, makes it apparent that some make the effort to talk and write about it anyway.

In spite of its fundamental ineffability, the experience is felt to be <u>overwhelmingly real</u>, even more real than the common reality of everyday life. The intuitive, mystical or ecstatic interlude takes one into a dimension of consciousness never before experienced. It is not intellectual in nature so it does not occur through the thinking mind, but instead floods one's entire being with a sudden (and what feels to be a certain) knowledge. It is the profound sense of the unquestionable realness of the experience that gives it the power to intervene in and alter the direction of one's life.

The Transforming Nature of the Field of Consciousness Experience

Ineffability is a characteristic of the experience that is problematic only if one cares to talk about it afterwards. Otherwise, it signals an absorption in a radically different dimension of consciousness where words are superfluous and something akin to "putting white paint on a white rose."

The characteristics of egolessness, unity, ineffability and realness combine to create an experience that offers a healthy counterbalance to the everyday tendency toward self-centeredness, and the taken-for-granted acceptance of a world carved out of pre-established labels and unquestioned definitions of what it means to be alive and human. When the experience occurs with any intensity, let alone regularity, it presents a view of the world and one's place in it so profoundly different than that to which one had grown accustomed

70

that an individual is brought up short and forced, as it were, to truly "see" that which has been placed before him.

The effect of this "seeing" is quite often enough to dramatically alter the manner in which a person subsequently pursues his or her life; from a competitive to a cooperative or complementary orientation, for example. Whereas prior to the onset of some intuitive interlude a person might not give a second thought to annihilating the better part of an ant colony with a couple of well-placed kicks in the earth, after such a moment wherein one realizes that all living things are expressions of the same field of consciousness, it might be unthinkable to disturb let alone destroy the same colony. Similarly, a religious or moral prescription like "do unto others" which once rattled with the emptiness of mere platitude now comes to resonate with meaning and purpose and provides a special sustenance otherwise unknown.

The transforming power of the field-of-consciousness experience stems from the radically different world-view of reality it offers, and the fact that this knowledge is transmitted all at once, without words, and is realized throughout the entire being of the individual. This is why it is such an effective antidote in counteracting the everyday tendency to label, compartmentalize, and judge.

Nothing short of the complementary experience of unity and selflessness will do if one is to check the tendency to live self-centeredly and so completely by labels and the unyielding distinctions and frozen meanings they create. The certain knowledge that all people share one and the same ultimate ground of Being transcends and overflows the usual sensation of I-centered separateness. The Western metaphysician Joel Goldsmith (1968) invites a consideration of the impact on behavior that the realization of oneness implies.

> But think what happens once you recognize that there is only one Being. That means that your being is my being, and therefore you cannot be good to me or bad to me; you can be to me only what you are to yourself. That is all!

In developing the intuitive side of the self we

71

stand to enriched ten-fold. Not only does one come to
experience the profound interrelatedness of the human
organism with the entire life process, but this experience creates the mind-set for the natural and spontaneous inclination to cooperate. It is the cultiva-
tion of this inclination to cooperate, it has been
argued, that will determine the degree of success
realized in managing the major international problems
that beset the world today. Having arrived at this
understanding, a particularly poignant question emerges
with significant implications for future research and
inquiry. For example, what responsibility do school
systems have to respond to the whole organism and develop the entire knowing potential of an individual?
The remarks that follow begin to speak to this question
and the changes in the approach to education that it
implies.

Conclusion:

Words as labels are the primary vehicle through
which the human animal is introduced to the on-going
world of meanings. This is a gradual process of becoming whereby human animality becomes civilized essentially by learning and internalizing the language
structure of a society. In this way one's awareness is
culturally conditioned, the house of one's consciousness is socially erected, but the scope and character
of one's vision is necessarily focused and narrowed.
Words introduce people to meaning, and to that end
they are essential. Ultimately, however, they are the
great delimiter of imagination and tend to keep people
locked within the parameters of intellectual definition
and description.

Both historically and currently, emphasis in
American schools has been to develop the left hemispheric abilities of the individual, known generally
as the "three basic R's", largely through teaching
techniques that both come from and appeal to the left
hemisphere as well. For a society with its educational
nose to the technological grindstone, nothing made
better sense throughout the industrial revolution than
to have the schools teach an objective "body of facts"
to a growing student clientele. In an era that spawn-
ed increasing complexity the specialist was born,
allowing the intellect the opportunity to penetrate
some particular aspect or segment of a whole system of
knowledge in depth.

School systems are not to be criticized or faulted so much for what they have been doing, as for what they have neglected to do. It is not fundamentally a matter of changing what is being done but rather of adding to it. In directing so much attention to the development of the intellect, schools have overlooked the intuitive dimension of human being and have thus addressed themselves to only one side of a living, multi-dimensional self. In so doing, they tend to take the life out of learning by confining it to the level of logic and reason. The Chinese scholar Siu (1957) offered the following observations regarding the responsibility of the schools to educate the whole person.

> In addition to thinking, the student should be provided with the education of feeling. He should not be led into the abject slavery of formal logic and rationality. He should be untethered from the restrictions of verbal and written symbols. He should learn to transcend language, sharing the sensitivities of St. Thomas, who as he wearily put aside his great treatise, the Summa Theologica, said it was 'all straw' (Siu, 1957).

The commitment of the schools can be expanded to include holistic growth and development where the full capacity of the individual to learn and know is nurtured and cared for. In addition to the "hard facts" of life, the student can also be introduced to some of the "soft" ones. For example, that the sure and certain demarcations and divisions of the world of appearance are fundamentally creations of the mind and senses imposed on an otherwise whole and inseparable unity. In this way the student's awareness can be extended into what the Buddhists call the suchness of nature where "the sound of the bell is heard before it rings and the flight of the bird is seen before it flies" (Siu, 1957). (Striking the bell creates its differentiation in the realm of the senses and the student misses the opportunity to sense that which underlies it and remains undifferentiated.)

Similarly, in categorizing and compartmentalizing the world through the intellect, one can lose touch with its fluidity and ultimate uncertainty. The effort to capture the flow of life in neat verbal containers is bound to be frustrated and ultimately generate conflict in an age that has produced modern theoretical physics and the world-view it offers. The eminent physicist Werner Heisenberg maintains that as a result of modern physics the world is classified:

> . . . not into different groups of
> objects but into different groups
> of connections . . . . The world
> thus appears as a complicated tissue
> of events, in which connections of
> different kinds alternate or overlap
> or combine and thereby determine
> the texture of the whole (Heisenberg,
> 1958).

It is ever more apparent that to approach the understanding of this complicated tissue of events exclusively through the intellect ignores the complexity and fine shadings that constitute the "suchness" of life. The inadequacy of this approach stems from its being incomplete and thus inaccurate. In and of itself, the world is not differentiated by hard and fast boundaries and in the same sense people, in and of themselves, are not what they have been labeled. There is simply more to it all than that; more subtlety, more in the way of intricate integration, more complexity.

In helping students to approach and understand the fact that the world and its events are ultimately woven in a continuous tissue rather than separated by discrete distinctions, the basis for tolerance is established. People may not be as quick to judge and condemn the unorthodox or unconventional thoughts and behavior of others if they genuinely know this to be the natural and inevitable way of life. Siu (1957) has suggested that ". . . strange ideas are tolerated in the light of the knowledge that complexity and variation are quite natural."

This approach to education and understanding has been largely overlooked and omitted from school methodologies and curricula. This omission is especially significant in view of the commonly taken metaphysical position that true unselfish, unconditional love and regard for others begins to root and flower in the intuitive, holistic, field-of-consciousness experience. J. Krishnamurti, one of the most internationally respected of the Eastern metaphysicians, put the point with the clarity and simplicity that has come to be associated with his discourses.

> We see the ways of the intellect but
> we do not see the way of love. The
> way of love is not to be found through
> the intellect. The intellect, with
> all its ramifications, with all its
> desires, ambitions, pursuits, must
> come to an end for love to come into
> existence . . . The moment I begin
> to think, to have ideas, opinions
> about it, I am already in a state of
> distraction, looking away from the
> thing I must understand . . . . Don't
> you know that when you love, you
> cooperate, you are not thinking of your
> self? That is the highest form of
> intelligence. When your vested
> interests are there, there can be no
> love; there is only the process of
> exploitation, born of fear. So love
> can come into being only when the
> mind is not there. Therefore you
> must understand the whole process of
> the mind, the function of the mind
> (J. Krishnamurti, 1970).

The function of the mind, it has been proposed here,
is bimodal in nature. There is the capacity to know
about the world through the intellect and the concepts
it generates which mediate the relationship between
people and the objective world of events. Additionally,
however, the process of conceptualization functions to
color perceptions and construct realities based on the
language-meaning structures of a society. The nature
of the knowledge that results is typically linear,
culturally relative, and therefore subject to a variety
of limitations in depth and dimension.

There is also the capacity to know the world
intuitively and directly, unencumbered by language and
thought. Whereas intellectual knowledge is largely a
step-by-step cerebral expression of the mind, intuitive
knowing manifests as an immediate apprehension of the
whole realized throughout the total human organism. It,
therefore, involves an intimate communion with the
known that is deep and abiding and thus adds an essential quality or dimension of awareness to the process
of knowing and being.

Rather than being at odds, these two modes of knowing actually imply and complement one another. To have one without the other creates a state of deficiency and imbalance that is dysfunctional and ultimately unnecessary since mind is a holism that incorporates both. Clearly, it is possible to have the best of each of these worlds where intuitive insight is continually making transparent the horizons created by the effort to describe and define the human experience.

BIBLIOGRAPHY

Adler, Mortimer and Robert Hutchins. ed. The Great
    Ideas Today 1970. New York: Encyclopedia
    Britanica. 1970

Allman, Lawrence R. and Dennis T. Jaffe. Readings in
    Abnormal Psychology: Contemporary Perspectives.
    New York: Harper and Row. 1976.

Asimov, Isaac. The Human Brain Its Capacities and
    Functions. Boston: Houghton Mifflin Company,
    Inc. 1963.

Assagioli, Roberto. Psychosyntheses: A Manual of
    Principles and Techniques. Hobbs, Dorman, and
    Company, Inc. 1971.

Baba, Mehr. God to Man and Man to God. North Myrtle
    Beach: Sheridan Press. 1975.

Becker, Howard S. Outsiders. New York: The Free
    Press. 1973.

Berger, Peter L. The Social Construction of Reality.
    Garden City: Doubleday and Company, Inc. 1967.

Bogen, Joseph E. "The Other Side of The Brain: An
    Oppositional Mind." Bulletin of the Los Angeles
    Neurological Societies, 34, No. 3, July 1969,
    135-62.

Bohr, Neils. Atomic Physics and Human Knowledge. New
    York: Wiley. 1958.

Bohr, Neils. Essays, 1958-1962, on Atomic Physics and
    Human Knowledge. New York: Wiley. 1963.

Brophy, Jere and Thomas Good. "Teachers' Communications
    of Differential Expectations for Children's
    Classroom Performance." Journal of Educational
    Psychology, 61, 5, 365-74. 1970.

Brown, B. "The Assessment of Self Concept Among Four
    Year Old Negro and White Children: A Compara-
    tive Study Using the Brown ID's Self-Concept
    Reference Test." New York: Institution of
    Developmental Studies. 1968.

77

Bruner, Jerome. "On Perceptual Readiness." Psychological Review, 64, 123-52. 1957.

Buber, Martin. I and Thou. New York: Charles
Scribner's Sons. 1970,

Bucke, Richard M, Cosmic Consciousness, New York:
E, P. Dunton and Company, Inc. 1969.

Burke, Kenneth. Language and Symbolic Action.
Berkeley: University of California Press. 1966.

Buscaglia, Leo. Love. Greenwich: Fawcett Books.1972.

Campbell, Keith. Body and Mind. Garden City:
Doubleday and Company, Inc. 1970.

Carroll, J. B. ed. Language, Thought and Reality:
Selected Writings of Benjamin Lee Whorf.
Cambridge: The M.I.T. Press. 1956.

Castaneda, Carlos. The Teachings of Don Juan: A Yaqui
Way of Knowledge. New York: Ballantine Books.
1968.

Cave, William M. and Mark A. Chesler. Sociology of
Education. New York: MacMillan Publishers
Company, Inc. 1974.

Cicourel, Aaron V. and John I. Kitsuse. The Educational
Decision Makers. New York: The Bobbs-Merrill
Company, Inc. 1963.

Clausen, John A. ed. Socialization and Society.
Boston: Little, Brown and Co. 1968.

Clifford, M.M. and E. Walster. "The Effect of Physical
Attractiveness on Teacher Expectations."
Sociology of Education, 46, 248-58. 1973.

Crile, George Jr. The Naturalistic View of Man. New
York: The World Publishing Co. 1969.

Dass, Ram. Journey of Awakening: A Meditator's
Guidebook. New York: Bantam Books. 1978.

Davidson, H.H. and G. Lang. "Children's Perception of
Teachers' Feelings Toward Them." Journal of
Experimental Education, 29, 107-18. 1960.

78

de Chardin, Teilhard. The Phenomenon of Man. New York: Harper and Row. 1955.

Deikman, Arthur J. "Bimodal Consciousness." Archives of General Psychiatry, 25, 481-89. Dec. 1971. American Medical Association.

Deikman, Arthur J. "Deautomatization and the Mystic Experience." Psychiatry, 29, 324-38. 1966.

Derlega, Valarian J. and Alan Chaiken. Sharing Intimacy New Jersey: Prentice-Hall, Inc. 1975.

Dewey, John. Experience and Education. New YOrk: Collier Books. 1938.

Drews, Elizabeth M. and Leslie Liopson. Values and Humanity. New York: St. Martin's Press. 1975.

Faris, Robert E. ed. Handbook of Modern Sociology. Chicago: Rand McNally and Company, Inc. 1964.

Ferguson, Marilyn. The Brain Revolution. New York: Taplinger Publishing Co. 1973.

Flanders, Ned and S. Havumaki. "The Effect of Teacher-Pupil Contacts Involving Praise on the Socio-metric Choices of Students." Journal of Education Psychology, 51, 65-68. 1960.

Fuller, R. Buckminster. Intuition. Garden City: Doubleday and Co. 1970.

Gazzaniga, Michael S. "The Split Brain in Man." Scientific American, 217 No. 2 Aug. 1967. 24-29.

Glass, John F. and John R. Staude. ed. Humanistic Society. Pacific Pallisades: Goodyear Publishing Company, Inc.

Goaldman, L. "Counseling Methods and Techniques: The Use of Tests," in The Encyclopeida of Education. ed. by I.C. Deighton. New York: MacMillian Publishers Company, Inc. 1971.

Goffman, Erving. Stigma. Englewood Cliffs: Prentice-Hall, Inc. 1963.

Goffman, Erving. The Presentation of Self in Everyday Life. Garden City: Doubleday and Company, Inc. 1959.

Goldsmith, Joel S. Beyond Words and Thoughts. Secaucus: The Citidel Press. 1968.

Hastorf, Albert H. and Hadley Cantril. "They Saw A Game: A Case Study." Journal of Abnormal Social Psychology, 49, Jan. 1945. 129-34.

Heise, David R. Personality and Socialization. Chicago: Rand McNally and Co. 1972.

Heisenberg, Werner. Physics and Philosophy. New York: Harper and Bros. 1958.

Henry, Jules. Culture Against Man. New York: Random House. 1963.

Hewitt, John P. Self and Society: A Symbolic Interactionist Social Psychology. Boston: Allyn and Bacon, Inc. 1976.

Hobard, Billie. Expansion. New York: Glenco Press. 1973.

Husserl, Edmund. Ideas (Translated by Boyce Gibson). New York: MacMillan. 1931.

Husserl, Edmund. Phenomenology and the Crises of Philosophy. New York: Harper and Row. 1965.

Huxley, Aldous. The Doors of Perception. New York: Harper and Row. 1954.

Ittelson, W.H. and F.P. Kilpatrick. "Experiments in Perception." Scientific American, 185, Aug. 1951. 50-55.

James, William. The Principles of Psychology. New York: Henry Holt. 1890.

James, William. The Varieties of Religious Experience. New York: Modern Library. 1929.

Johnson, J. "On The Interface Between Low-Income Urban Black Children and Their Teachers During The Early School Years.": A Position Paper. San Francisco: for West Laboratory for Educational

Research and Development. 1973.

Jourard, Sidney M. The Transparent Self. Princeton:
    D. Van Nostrand. 1974.

Keen, Sam. Voices and Visions. New York: Harper and
    Row. 1970.

King, Edith W. Education of Young Children, Sociological
    Interpretations. Dubuque: Wm. C. Brown Company
    Publishers. 1973.

Krishnamurti, J. Commentaries on Living: First Series.
    Wheaton: The Theosophical Publishing House.
    1956.

Krishnamurti, J. The Awakening of Intelligence. New
    York: Avon Books. 1973.

Krishnamurti, Jr. Think on These Things. New York:
    Perennial Library, Harper and Row. 1970.

Laing, R.D. The Politics of Experience. New York:
    Ballantine. 1967.

Lauer, Robert H. and Warran H. Handel. Social Psychol-
    ogy: The Theory and Application of Symbolic
    Interactionism. Boston: Houghton Mifflin Co.
    1977.

Le Shan, Lawrence. How to Meditate. New York: Bantam
    Books. 1974.

Le Shan, Lawrence. The Medium The Mystic and The
    Physicist. New York: Viking Press. 1974.

Mackler, B. "Grouping in the Ghetto." Education and
    Urban Society, 2, 80-95. 1969.

Manheim, Karl. Ideology and Utopia. London: Routledge
    and Kegan Paul. 1936.

Mannis, Jerome G. and Bernard W. Meltzer. ed. Symbolic
    Interactions. Boston: Allyn and Bacon, Inc.
    1972.

Matson, Floyd W. The Broken Image. Garden City:
    Anchor Books. 1966.

May, Rolo. _Man's Search for Himself._ New York:
　　W. W. Norton and Co. 1953.

Mead, George H. _Mind, Self and Society._ Chicago:
　　University of Chicago Press. 1956.

Nisbit, Robert A. _Emile Durkheim._ New Jersey:
　　Prentice-Hall, Inc. 1968.

Ornstein, Robert E. ed. _The Nature of Human Conscious-
　　ness._ San Francisco: W.H. Freeman and Co.
　　1973.

Ornstein, Robert E. ed. _The Psychology of Conscious-
　　ness._ San Francisco: W.H. Freeman and Co.
　　1972.

Pavalki, Ronald M. _Sociology of Education: A Book of
　　Readings._ Illinois: F.E. Peacock Publishers,
　　Inc. 1968.

Penfield, Wilder. _The Mystery of the Mind._ Princeton:
　　Princeton University Press. 1975.

Phillips, Bernard. _Social Research, Strategy and
　　Tactics._ New York: The MacMillan Co. 1966.

Polanyi, Michael. _The Tacit Dimension._ Garden City:
　　Doubleday and Company, Inc. 1966.

Rajneesh, Bhagwan Shree. _Only One Sky: On the Tantric
　　Way of Tilopa's Song of Mahamudra._ New York:
　　E.P. Dutton. 1975.

Regush, Nicholas. ed. _Visibles and Invisibles._ Boston:
　　Little, Brown and Ci. 1973.

Rist, R.C. "Student Social Class and Teachers Expecta-
　　tions: The Self Fulfilling Prophecy in Ghetto
　　Education." _Harvard Educational Review_, 40,
　　411-50. 1970.

Rist, R.C. _The Urban School: A Factory for Failure._
　　Cambridge: The M.I.T. Press. 1973.

Rogers, Carl R. _On Becoming A Person._ Boston:
　　Houghton Mifflin Co. 1961.

Rosenthal, R. and L. Jacobson. Pygmalion in the Classroom. New York: Holt, Rinehart and Winston.
1968.

Rosenthal, R. and L. Jacobson. "Teacher's Expectancies:
Detriments of Pupils' I.Q. Gains." Psychology
Reports. 19, 115-18. 1966.

Rubin, Zick. Doing Unto Others. Englewood Cliffs:
Prentice-Hall. 1973.

Rubovits, P. and M. L. Maehr. "Pygmalion Black and
White." Journal of Personality and Social
Psychology, 2, 210-18. 1973.

Russel, Bertrand. The ABC of Relativity. New York:
Mentor Books. 1958.

Ryan, William. Blaming the Victims. New York:
Vintage Books. 1971.

Sagan, Carl. The Dragons of Eden. New York: Ballantine Books. 1977.

Scheff, Thomas. Labeling Madness. Englewood Cliffs:
Prentice-Hall. 1975.

Schmuck, Richard A. and Patricia A. Schmuck. A Humanistic Psychology of Education. National Press
Books. 1974.

Schur, Edwin M. Labeling Deviant Behavior. New York:
Harper and Row. 1971.

Schutz, Alfred. Collected Papers: The Problem of
Social Reality (Vol. I). ed. Maurice Natanson.
The Hague: Martinus Nijhoff. 1967.

Schwartz, Gerri E. ec. Annual Editions: Readings
in Personality and Adjustment 78-79. Guilford:
The Dushkin Publishing Group. 1978.

Sieber, Sam D. and David E. Wilder. The School in
Society. New York: Free Press. 1973.

Silberman, Charles W. Crisis in the Classroom: The
Remaking of American Education. New York:
Random House. 1970.

Singh, Darshan. <u>Sant Mat: The Teachings of the Masters</u>.
  Bowling Green: Sawan Kirpal Meditation Center.
  1977.

Siu, R.G.H. <u>The Tao of Science.</u> Cambridge: The M.I.T.
  Press. 1957.

Slater, Philip, <u>The Wayward Gate</u>. Boston: Beacon
  Press. 1977.

Sperry, R.W., M.S. Gazzaniga and J.E. Bogen. "Role of
  the Neo Cortical Commissures." In Vinken and
  Bruyn. Vol. IV. 1969.

Stein, A. "Strategies for Failure." <u>Harvard Educational Review</u>, 41, 158-204. 1971

Stone, Gregory P. and Harvey A. Farberman. <u>Social
  Psychology Through Symbolic Interactions.</u>
  London: Ginn-Blaisdell. 1970.

Strauss, Anselm. ed. <u>George Herbert Mead on Social
  Psychology.</u> Chicago: The University of
  Chicago Press. 1964.

Suzuki, D.T. ed. <u>Essays on Zen Buddism</u>. New York:
  Grove Press. 1946.

Volkart, Edmund H. <u>Social Behavior and Personality.</u>
  New York: Social Science Research Community.
  1951.

Vygotsky, L.S. <u>Thought and Language.</u> New York: M.I.T.
  Press and John Wileg and Sons, Inc. 1962.

Watts, Alan W. <u>Psychotherapy East and West.</u> New York:
  Mentor Books. 1961

Watts, Alan W. <u>The Book</u>. New York: MacMillan Co. 1966.

Watzlawick, Paul. How Real is Real?: <u>Confusion-Disin-
  formation-Communication.</u> New York: Random
  House. 1976.

White, Alan R. The Philosophy of Mind. New York:
  Random House. 1967.

Wilson, Everett. <u>Sociology</u>. Illinois: The Dorsey
  Press. 1971